CW00347039

VICTORIAN LEICESTER

VICTORIAN LEICESTER

by

MALCOLM ELLIOTT

PHILLIMORE

1979

Published by
PHILLIMORE & CO. LTD.,
London and Chichester
Head Office: Shopwyke Hall, Chichester,
Susssex, England

ISBN 0 85033 327 X

Printed in England by
UNWIN BROTHERS, LTD.,
at the Gresham Press, Old Woking, Surrey

and bound at
THE NEWDIGATE PRESS, LTD.,
Book House, Dorking, Surrey

To
Jennifer
Jonathan, Christopher
and Rebecca

CONTENTS

LIST OF PLATES

(*between pages 48 and 49*)

LIST OF TEXT ILLUSTRATIONS

PREFACE

Victorian achievements in technology and civil engineering continue to evoke some of the awe and fascination that they inspired in contemporaries. We marvel at physical monuments to man's ingenuity, such as bridges and viaducts, steam pumps and traction engines, with much the same respect for creative genius and inventive skill as excited the crowds who thronged Paxton's Crystal Palace. The visible wonders of the Victorian age perhaps make us blind to the more mundane aspects of its legacy to the present. In a review of municipal progress written in 1935, J. L. Hammond argued that a comparison of the state of towns at that time with their condition a century earlier would lead us to regard our system of local government as 'the greatest British achievement in the last hundred years'.[1] This book looks at how that system was achieved in Leicester. It is a study of the environmental problems which commanded the attention of the Victorians and which thereby determined the growing points in the machinery of local administration.

The phenomenal growth of urban population in the early 19th century strained, often beyond breaking point, the traditional means of drainage and water supply. These twin amenities were rightly regarded as fundamental to the maintenance of public health and it was to their improvement that sanitarian reformers of the mid-19th century directed most urgent attention. At the same time population pressure exerted a constant strain on living space. Houses encroached onto meadows, orchards and gardens, while in the dark interiors of towns every conceivable room was pressed into service as living accommodation. Each man pursuing his own interests did not always produce results conducive to the good of the community, and corporate limits had to be set both to the freedom to exploit and to suffer the consequences of such land hunger. So that readers may set local events into the national context of legislative change, I have summarised the development of English local government in the 19th century in an introductory chapter.

There then follows an essay on Leicester in the early 19th century which I trust will give the reader his bearings as the focus of attention moves to specific areas of town government.

Leicester has rarely engaged the attention of national historians, for it is neither typical of industrial centres, nor does it hold the charm of an ancient market town like Shrewsbury or Norwich, that escaped the ravages of Victorian rebuilding. Yet Leicester was both a market town of great antiquity and the scene of phenomenal industrial growth. Only one in seven of the county population lived in Leicester in 1801, but very nearly half did so 100 years later. Its citizens, from toiling in the poverty of a domestic system producing little except hosiery, had by the end of the century a wealth of light industries in which to earn their bread.

It is with this transformation and the attendant problems of housing, sanitation and social amenities that this book is concerned. My thanks are due to innumerable people who have helped me to write it. In particular, Mr. Rupert Evans of the Department of Modern History at Leicester University, Mr. Douglas Ashby, and my colleague, Mr. Peter Jones, who read drafts of the book and gave me valuable advice. The initial impetus to my writing came from Professor A. W. Coats and Dr. Helen Meller of the University of Nottingham, whose firm guidance enabled me to steer my way through the mass of material in the local Record Office while researching on the Leicester Board of Health. To these acknowledgments I must add the usual caveat that these good folk are in no way responsible for any imperfections that remain.

The photographs owe much to my friends Mr. Andrew Hollingbery and Mr. Ross Wallis, whose talents with a camera far exceed my own, and I am especially grateful to

Mr. Jack Jeffs of Scraptoft College who gave so generously of his time and skill to improve the quality of many of the illustrations. I wish to acknowledge a special debt to Mrs. Anne Gregson for her superb ink drawing, on page 138 and on the endpapers, of 'Elmfield', the house, now sadly demolished, that Samuel Stone had built for himself in 1848. Here he wrote his *Justices' Manual* and other works of reference. It is fitting that the home of one so close to the heart of civic affairs should feature at the beginning and end of a study on municipal progress in Victorian Leicester.

I would also like to thank the helpful assistants at the Leicestershire Record Office and the City Library and University Library and the staff of the University Cartographic department for their assistance. My thanks also to so many kind friends, such as the veteran local historian, Eric Swift, for inspiration and encouragement; to my excellent typist, Mrs. Margaret Phillipson, and finally to my wife and family for suffering my absorption with Leicester's history; to them this book is affectionately dedicated.

MALCOLM ELLIOTT

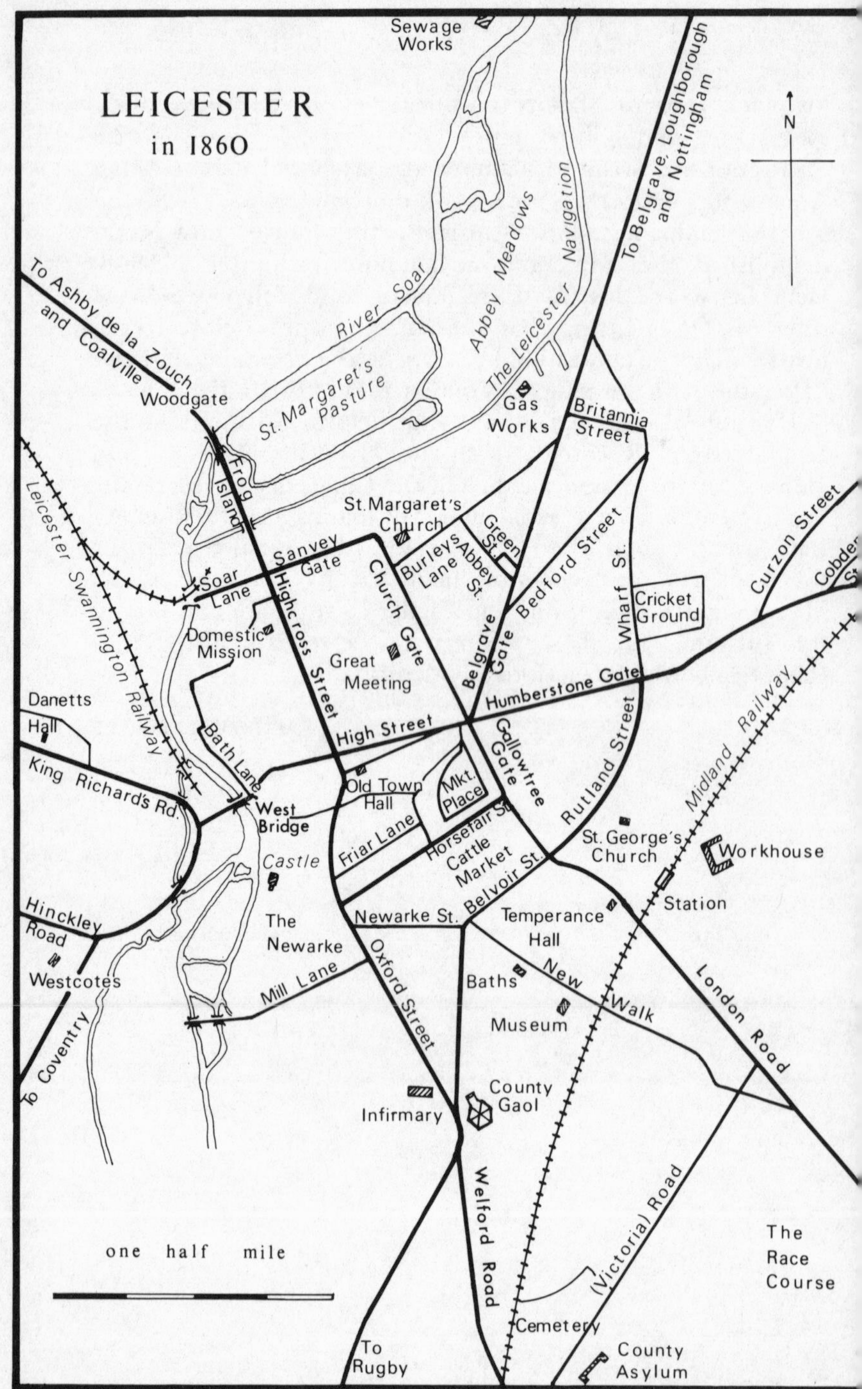

Fig. 1. Map of Leicester showing places mentioned in the text

INTRODUCTION

ENGLISH LOCAL GOVERNMENT as it exists today is still largely a product of the Victorian period. In the early 19th century there was a bewildering assortment of administrative authorities, some dating from the remote past and others created to meet the need for urban improvement and rural transport as England felt the first impact of the Industrial Revolution. The hundreds and shires, the justices in Quarter Sessions, the parish vestries and chartered corporations in towns, courts baron and courts leet, co-existed in varying degrees of harmony with sundry bodies of commissioners for policing, lighting and paving, with Poor Law Unions and Turnpike Trusts and other *ad hoc* creations.[1]

Administration in rural areas remained in the hands of the unpaid justices of the peace throughout most of the 19th century. Their judicial functions had gradually developed to include responsibility for ensuring that roads and bridges were kept in repair, that the overseers of the poor discharged their duties efficiently and that law and order were preserved. In the Tudor period, the magistrates had become not only judicial beasts of burden, but administrative maids of all work,[2] and with the weakening of central control in the 17th century their power and status in rural society increased further. In the towns many of their administrative functions were vested in the corporate authorities and the division of responsibility was often disputed.[3]

The only common element in administrative areas throughout the country was the parish. It was natural, therefore, that when utilitarian reformers turned their attention to the establishment of a new framework of local administration, it was the parishes that they naturally regarded as the basis upon which to build an ordered system,[4] and within the parishes it was to the most expensive and burdensome obligation of local government, the administration of the Poor Law, that their reforming principles were first applied.

In 1830, widespread outbreaks of machine-smashing and rick-burning had dramatically drawn attention to discontent among the labouring poor of rural England. Low wages and scarcity of employment, exacerbated by the incipient threat of machinery, drove men and women from all over the agricultural districts of south and central England to the desperate expedient of clandestine attacks on property in the name of the fictitious 'Captain Swing'.[5] Poverty may even have been created by the very system designed to relieve it. The so-called Speenhamland system which gave monetary assistance in proportion to the price of bread and the size of the labourer's family, does not appear to have been so widely practised as it was once thought to have been, but some form of addition to the wages of free labourers in proportion to the size of their families was almost universal in the south and east of England. It was thought, however erroneously, that these rates in aid of wages depressed the free market price of labour and made dependence on the parish the inescapable lot of many farm labourers. Public charity, it was argued, served to discourage the poor from earning their own living and added thereby to the level of unemployment.[6]

Thus the natural desire of the propertied classes to reduce expenditure on poor relief, which averaged six and three-quarter million pounds in the years 1830 to 1834, was given theoretical and moral justification.[7] Cutting allowances to the unemployed was disguised as a move to restore the self-respect and independence of the poor.

Economy and efficiency in administration of poor relief were the primary objectives of the parliamentary commissioners appointed in 1833 to enquire into the working of the Poor Law. Their report of the following year envisaged the creation of a central body of Poor Law Commissioners presiding over locally-elected Boards of Guardians, who were henceforth to operate the Poor Laws.

The administrative machinery of the New Poor Law thus bore a striking resemblance to the legislative framework advocated by Jeremy Bentham in his Constitutional Code.[8] Bentham had not in fact published this work when he died in 1832, but none knew the mind of the master more intimately than his private secretary and confidant, Edwin Chadwick. Together with Nassau Senior, the economist, he drafted the report of the Commission and after the passage of the Amendment Act, became Secretary to the Poor Law Commission. Bentham envisaged a system of district governments or sub-legislatures, each exercising control within its field over taxation, expenditure and public services such as education as well as poor relief. In creating his unions of parishes under the central Commission of the Poor Law, Chadwick was therefore embarking on the first step towards what might have become a Benthamite system of local government covering every aspect of administation. Indeed, when the registration of births, marriages and deaths came into operation three years later it was entrusted to these same authorities; and when Chadwick turned his attention to sanitation it was once again to the Guardians that he looked for the administration of the first legislation on public health in the Nuisance Removal Act of 1846; the precedent was followed in 1866 when the Guardians were designated as the nuisance removal authorities in rural areas throughout the country.

Under the Poor Law Amendment Act all relief was to be given within the workhouses, and outdoor relief was forbidden except in extreme cases of need. The certification of medical grounds for such out relief led to one of the most constructive innovations of the period, namely the institution of Poor Law medical officers, whose reports later proved an invaluable source of first-hand information on the state of the poor.[9]

Any claimant who failed to convince the medical officer of the imperative need for help in his own home, was 'offered the House', that is to say, given the option of entering the workhouse or making do without any assistance; and, in case the evils should seem too nicely balanced, the new workhouses were to be conducted on such spartan lines as would deter all but the most desperate from claiming relief. Idlers and malingerers were thus to be forced onto the free labour market and removed from the arena of public charity.

This was, however, the limit of Chadwick's achievement in attempting to reorganise English local government on the basis of the Poor Law Unions. The experiment might have been more extensive if it had not been so effective in dealing with pauperism or if it had begun in some other sphere, for such was the hatred and obloquy attendant on the Poor Law Commission and their 'bastilles' that there was no chance of linking further extensions of local government to the existing system.[10] The reform of local administration in succeeding years therefore followed no Benthamite utilitarian vision of universality, but took the form of a piecemeal attack upon particular facets of the existing complex of local institutions.

In 1832 parliament had swept away much of the accumulated debris that choked its own effectiveness as a representative body, and it was hardly surprising that it should turn its attention in the following year to the reform of government within the ancient boroughs of the realm. Not only was there a parallel case for extending the principle of elected representation and for uniformity in their administration, but they were, for the most part, bastions of Tory power which had exercised a powerful influence in the choice of borough M.P.s. The enquiry into the government of municipal corporations was not therefore without political motivation. The commissioners chosen were mostly able young barristers of Whig or radical persuasion, whose task was rather to substantiate the case against the old corporations than to present any balanced view of their effectiveness. Their report was in consequence a damning indictment of the existing system as inefficient, corrupt and unrepresentative.[11]

The commissioners examined 246 towns with little in common except their legal status as corporations and their right to hold property, a right which as Lord Eldon pointed out, gave them the power to dispose of such property just as individuals could dispose of theirs.[12] Almost all the old corporations were in the habit of holding lavish dinners for the enjoyment of the common council at the expense of corporate funds. At Berwick-on-Tweed the commissioners even found the freemen had 'borrowed money expressly for the purpose of dividing it amongst themselves'.[13]

That the commissioners would condemn the confusion that confronted them was a foregone conclusion. There was little attempt at impartial and dispassionate assessment of the old system; instead they declared that 'the existing municipal corporations of England and Wales neither possess nor deserve the confidence and respect of your Majesty's subjects'. In seeking out evidence to condemn the old corporations, the commissioners found Leicester a remarkably rich quarry. Bribery, peculation and gross inefficiency could hardly have been more blatant or more openly acknowledged than in the records relating to the borough in the decade prior to 1835. Consequently, when reform came to Leicester its impact was as damning to the old régime as it was propitious for its critics.

The Municipal Reform Act which received the Royal Assent in September 1835, applied only to 179 boroughs in England and Wales, and their combined population represented only a seventh of the total inhabitants of the country at that time. The Act did not lead to any great extension in the work of the corporations. Their sphere of operation and conception of their duties did not radically differ from the traditional view. The only major obligation placed upon the new corporations was the setting up of Watch Committees to supervise the conduct of efficient police forces. Apart from this, the change was largely confined to administrative standards of efficiency. The new councils were to be elected by ratepayers resident in the town for three years. One third of the council was to retire or seek re-election each year. A conservative amendment led to the retention of aldermen, who comprised one quarter of the whole council and were chosen by the elected members themselves for a period of six years. This ancient office dating back to Saxon times thus survived until the Conservative government of Mr. Heath swept them out of existence in 1974. Council meetings were to be opened to the public and the accounts of the treasurer and town clerk had to be audited once a year. Corporate property was thenceforth to be used for the 'benefit of the inhabitants and the improvement of the borough' and not for the private interests of individuals.[16]

The Act of 1835 did not attempt any such centralised or uniform pattern of administration as Chadwick had imposed on the New Poor Law. Apart from requiring Treasury approval for the raising of capital or sale of corporate property, Westminster left the corporations fully possessed of their cherished independence. There was moreover no attempt to vest the new councils with omnipotence within their own boundaries. The Highways Act passed in the same year put maintenance of the roads under the charge of salaried Surveyors of Highways appointed by the parish vestries.[17] Populous parishes might under this Act constitute separate Highways Boards, while others could if they wished apply for permission to combine with their neighbours to form Highway Districts. The variety of administrative units thus proliferated; instead of single all-purpose local authorities there developed a multiplicity of separate bodies to carry out specific functions of local government.

After 1848, Local Boards of Health were established to look after the sanitary needs of the towns. By the Act of 1852, Burial Boards could be set up by either the vestry or the council to supervise and maintain burial grounds. Following the Forster Act of 1870, School Boards were established with elections quite different from those for the ordinary council. The functions of Health and Burial Boards were thus assumed by the existing corporate authorities, while the provision of education and the relief of poverty were everywhere the preserve of *ad hoc* bodies. In some cases this led to conflicts of interest and differences of opinion over the division of responsibility.

In Leeds, the Board of Guardians retained its control over sanitary measures in default of action by the local authority, and actually indicted the council on account of the condition of one of its properties. It was not until 1865 that this conflict was resolved when the Leeds Council assumed the responsibilties of the Guardians for the removal of nuisances.[18] In Birmingham, Street Commissioners held sway under the authority of five successive Acts between 1769 and 1828; and by 1851 there were eight different bodies responsible for local government in the town.[19] The Municipal Corporations Act had given the new corporations no power to assume control over the existing special authorities and it was not until the Improvement Act of 1851 that the Corporation of Birmingham finally established its supremacy as the principal local authority.[20]

How effective these various Street and Improvement Commissions were, it is difficult to judge. They worked with limited resources, limited knowledge and a limited conception of their own duties.[21] They had come into existence mainly during the late 18th century to deal with particular and specific local problems such as bad road surfaces or inadequate drainage. Frequently their funds were exhausted and they had levied their maximum permitted rates before their work of 'paving, cleansing, lighting, sewering, watching and generally improving' had properly begun.[22] The technical difficulties of town drainage alone were scarcely understood until the mid-19th century. Nevertheless, the Webbs conclude that 'such work as was done by the Improvement Commissioners was a clear gain to the community. Their sins were sins of omission. It passes human imagination to conceive the state into which the rapidly-growing towns would have got if no such bodies had been established'.[23]

Advocates of urban sanitation in the early 19th century faced almost insuperable obstacles. Industrial towns often grew at 30 or 40 per cent. per decade. Bradford, at the heart of the Yorkshire woollen industry, increased by 69 per cent. between 1821 and 1831.[24] Such growth rates made it well-nigh impossible for existing drains and sewers to suffice and for the most part, these had always been inadequate.

The disposal of domestic sewage was normally effected by means of a cesspit dug in the back yard or garden. The increasing provision of water closets from about 1820 greatly added to the volume of matter to be disposed of, overflowing cesspools were a frequent source of complaint, and not infrequently their proximity to wells infected the domestic water supply. Sometimes cesspools were actually built in the basements of houses; Windsor Castle contained 53 such cesspools in 1850, all of them full and overflowing.[25]

The stench from such contrivances must have been odious in the extreme and to contemporaries this was not merely a matter of smell, but of life and death, for the current medical orthodoxy held that bad air was the cause of disease and death. 'All smell is disease', Chadwick roundly declared.[26] It was this so-called pythogenic theory that led him to regard public nuisances, such as unclean streets, as a root cause of poverty. Insanitary conditions led to debility, sickness and death. These in turn led men to seek help from the Poor Law authorities and ultimately threw their widows and children into the workhouse.

In 1838, acting on the advice of their medical officers, the Guardians of some London Poor Law Unions undertook to remove some of the more obvious health hazards in order to effect an ultimate saving in expenditure on poor relief. The government auditors, however, disallowed this expenditure on the grounds that the Poor Law Amendment Act did not authorise spending money on such purposes.[27]

As a result of this decision the Poor Law Commissioners set in motion an enquiry into the environmental causes of ill-health in the metropolis. Their report issued in May 1938 was a forerunner of Chadwick's much wider enquiry into sanitary conditions. Chadwick relied heavily on the information supplied to him by the medical officers of the Poor Law Unions. In July 1842 his 'Report on the Sanitary Condition of the Labouring Population' was published under his own name.[28] It contained a mass of evidence on the insufficiency of sewers, the gross overcrowding of labourers' dwellings, the pollution of water supplies and the moral and physical degeneration of the people condemned to live in such conditions. Chadwick's basic remedies were the supply of fresh piped water and the efficient disposal of sewage.

By one of those fortunate accidents of history, sanitary reform became the question of the hour just when earthenware manufacturers were able to put glazed pipes on to the market at progressively lower prices. Instead of the old flat and irregular sewers constructed of brick and big enough for men to walk through, Chadwick advocated smooth pipes small enough to carry water-borne sewage at a velocity sufficient to make them self-cleansing.[29]

Despite the success of his report in rousing public opinion to the importance of drainage and water supply and despite the additional evidence gathered by Slaney's Committee on the Health of Towns,[30] which sat and reported in 1840 while Chadwick's own enquiry was still proceeding, no official action resulted for four years. Instead, Peel's government took the line of least resistance and appointed a royal commission under the Duke of Buccleuch to investigate the issues once again and to suggest detailed legislation.

The commission reported in 1844 and 1845 suggesting a comprehensive public health Bill and giving further detailed evidence on the state of large towns.[31] Published at the height of the Irish potato famine and its reverberations on English politics, the report did not lead to any immediate action. Only the relatively minor Nuisances Removal Act of 1846 can be seen as the direct consequence of all this volume of evidence in official reports. This Act was intended to facilitate attention to sanitary deficiences by Boards of Guardians, but in some instances it was operated by the reformed town councils as in Nottingham and Leicester. Indeed, Nottingham Council regarded its own achievements in this sphere as so efficacious as to remove any need to apply the Public Health Act of 1848.[32] In Leicester, the consequences of the Nuisances Removal Act were even more important, for not only was it the forerunner of action under the Public Health Acts, but it led directly to an administrative development of the greatest importance, namely the institution of the first Medical Officers by a local authority in England.

Chadwick in the meantime was busy promoting his Health of Towns Association, a sort of support society for the sanitarian reformers in local and national government. At the same time, his hope of prodding the local authorities into action in the matter of water supply and drainage was so far weakened as to lead him to float his own private company for the improvement of towns. Aided by Lord Francis Egerton, Dr. Arnott, Nassau Senior and Rowland Hill as fellow directors, the Towns Improvement Company attempted to raise capital for commercial undertakings in Leicester and elsewhere. The company failed in 1846 with the collapse of business confidence that followed the 'railway mania', but its flotation explains the clause in the Public Health Act, when it passed into law two years later, forbidding local authorities to set up their own water companies where such could be left to the action of private enterprise.[33] It was a stipulation curiously at odds with Chadwick's professed preference for municipal enterprise.

The most decisive influence upon sanitary thinking in the 1830s was undoubtedly the cholera epidemic of 1831-2. Asa Briggs has shown this to have been a European epidemic which roused local and central governments into a spate of active intervention.[34]

Most of the official reaction was confined to common-sense measures of advice to remove dirt and refuse, to change damp clothes, eat well-boiled vegetables and meat—advice which must have sounded somewhat hollow to the poor. The City of London Board of Health stated that cholera was a disease which 'falls with the greatest severity on the poor, the ill-fed and the unhealthy; and which rages most destructively in those districts of towns where the streets are narrow and the population crowded, and where little attention has been paid to cleanliness and ventilation'.[35] The association of the spread of disease with insanitary conditions was assumed beyond doubt. It was confidently stated as 'the opinion of all who witnessed the disease, that it was by no means contagious'.[36] One is reminded of the conduct of Dr. Southwood Smith who took his granddaughter with him on his tours of the hospital wards to demonstrate his disbelief in contagion as opposed to the pythogenic theory of causation of disease.[37]

As the epidemic passed, public reaction to cholera subsided and left no permanent trace. The local Boards of Health, such as that set up in Leicester, were disbanded. But the memory of the ravages of cholera proved a valuable aid to sanitary reform when the disease reappeared in 1847, and it gave a decisive push to the administrative machine that Chadwick was labouring to set in motion.

In 1847 Lord Morpeth, chief among the Whig advocates of sanitation reform, introduced a Bill for the promoting of public health. It was a measure that at once raised alarm among the defenders of local autonomy and it was rejected by the Commons. In the next session Morpeth introduced a revised version of his Bill with the timely support of cholera. On this occasion the remedial measures were to be more lasting. Parliament decided that the time had come to establish a permanent network of local boards linked to a central Board of Health in London, much as the Poor Law Commission exercised control over the local Boards of Guardians.

It was thus partly because of cholera and partly through the tireless efforts of Edwin Chadwick that English local government took its most decisive step since the reform of municipal corporations; for in setting up local boards and promoting through them the control of building, the cleaning of streets, the laying of drains and sewers, the provision of water supplies and the removal of health hazards, the Public Health Act laid the basis upon which most of the duties of local authorities now rest. The Act, however, fell far short of the Benthamite vision of a centralised and uniform system of sanitary authorities. It could only be applied if more than one-tenth of the ratepayers asked for it, if the council applied for its adoption, or if the death rate exceeded 23 per 1,000, in which case the General Board of Health might itself instigate moves. In practice this power of compulsion was rarely used.[38] In Manchester, Birmingham and Nottingham, for example, the town councils made clear their resentment toward interference by the central government and the Act was not applied despite the high death rates that prevailed in all these places.

By 1853, local boards had been established in 164 instances, only 28 of them requiring the compulsory powers of the General Board.[39] In the six years of its existence the Board was able to advise on a great many practical and efficient schemes of drainage and water supply and to guide the local boards through much of the routine work of sanitary improvement. But Chadwick's occasional errors of judgement, his arrogance and tactlessness served to turn opinion against the Board, and its effective life came to an end in 1854. Under the control of a president, the Board, on which there were effectively no other members, continued till 1858 when it was dissolved altogether. The medical duties of the Board were thereafter in the hands of the Privy Council. In effect the mantle of Chadwick had fallen since 1855 upon the able shoulders of Sir John Simon, as Medical Officer to the Privy Council.[40] It was partly through his conscientious reports and careful supervision that progress in preventive medicine continued to be made at a local level.

The non-medical functions of the Board of Health were transferred in 1858 to the newly-created Local Government Act Office. The cacophonous title refers to the Act passed in the same year for regulating the government of towns not covered by the Municipal Reform Act. It incorporated the provisions of the Public Health Act of 1848 and so constituted one of the major instalments of enabling legislation. Nottingham immediately adopted the Act, and proceeded at once to appoint its first Borough Surveyor, to issue regulations on the erection of new buildings and to extend the work of its earlier Sanitary Committee.[41] It did not, however, see fit to appoint a Medical Officer of Health until obliged to do so by the Local Government Board set up under Gladstone's Act of 1872.[42] Smaller authorities were even more tardy in accepting the need for such an appointment. Hinckley, in south-west Leicestershire, which did not adopt the 1858 Act until 10 years later, decided at one of its first meetings to defer the appointment of a medical officer 'sine die'.[43] When eventually they were nudged into action by the Local Government Board they advertised for the services of a suitably qualified person at £20 per annum, and when no-one accepted this offer they resolved to appoint 'on the best terms possible'.[44]

Tamworth, in Staffordshire, utterly refused to undertake any measures of sanitary reform whatever, despite its alarming death rate.[45]

It was this kind of complacency and inaction that prompted a renewed pressure for centralised control over public health. The call came particularly from two speakers to the National Association for the Promotion of Social Science, Dr. Alexander Stewart and a barrister, Edward Jenkins. Their papers on the 'Medical and Legal Aspects of Sanitary Reform', published in 1866, were a powerful plea for more rigorous action by the central government to promote elementary standards of health and hygiene by making the appointment of medical officers mandatory on all local authorities.[46] Throughout the book runs a naïve faith in the causal connection between the appointment of qualified health officers and the reduction of mortality from disease. The principle of compulsion by the central government was clearly re-established in the Sanitary Act of 1866, which obliged Boards of Guardians to deal with public nuisances and laid upon chief constables the duty of taking proceedings in default of such attention by the Guardians. The Secretary of State was authorised to undertake neglected works at the expense of the local authority if it failed to respond to instructions to rectify the situation.

In practice, however, the government was very reluctant to compel local authorities to act. The weakness of central control was exemplified in the position at Tamworth. Repeated warnings and pleas met with the adamant refusal of the local vestry to have anything to do with such unnecessary extravagances as sewerage and water supply. The clerk to the Tamworth Poor Law Guardians put the matter bluntly to the government: 'You must make up your mind, that except under pressure, the vestry will simply do nothing at all'.[47] Arthur Taylor, the government inspector sent to Tamworth, resigned himself to the truth of this view: 'If the action of the central authorities is confined to writing letters and remonstrances, I am of the opinion that such had better not be sent, as they only tend to bring that authority into contempt', he wrote. If compulsion could not be used, he said, 'the effect will be as bad on Boards of Guardians, as vestries and local authorities. The latter will soon hear that they can offend with impunity—the former will quickly grow tired of interfering with local authorities who can set the law at defiance'.[48]

In 1868 Disraeli set up a commission to enquire into the working of the Sanitary Acts. On the fall of his ministry a few weeks later, Gladstone replaced this with a new commission under C. B. Adderley, which reported in 1871. It was this report that prompted Goschen's remark about 'a chaos as regards authorities, a chaos as regards rates, and a worse chaos than all as regards areas'.[49] It was left to Stansfeld, Goschen's successor at the Poor Law Board, to implement Adderley's recommendation by setting up rural sanitary authorities based on the Boards of the Poor Law Guardians. Stansfeld also put through a Bill which created the new Local Government Board covering the work of the old Poor Law Board, the General Register Office, the Local Government Department of the Home Office and the Medical Department of the Privy Council. To sanitary reformers the reorganisation was a disaster, for the new board was heavily coloured by the experience and attitudes of the Poor Law administration. The public health lobby was now without an independent voice in the counsels of government, forced into union with a department dedicated to economy and the lingering orthodoxy of the Poor Law Amendment Act. This administrative misalliance was not ended until the formation of the Ministry of Health in 1919.

Disraeli's Act of 1875 confirmed the role of Poor Law Unions as rural sanitary authorities, so that by the last quarter of the 19th century Bentham's vision of a uniform structure of local administration under central government control was achieved so far as public health was concerned. In all other respects, however, the countryside was still governed as it had been for centuries, by the magistrates in Quarter Sessions. Repeated attempts to bring rural districts under democratic and representative government foundered in parliamentary committees or were withdrawn earlier. As Halevy pointed out, the Poor Law Amendment Act had removed from the justices' control their most odious function and given it to elected Guardians.[50] The principle of elected representation was not thereby enhanced, while the gentry who sat on the bench were never more popular.

The work of Joseph Arch in establishing a Union of Agricultural Labourers in 1872 and the passing of the third Reform Bill which gave agricultural workers the vote in 1884, brought renewed pressure for the democratisation of government in the counties. Sir Charles Dilke had formulated a thoroughgoing plan as President of the Local Government Board in Gladstone's second ministry. A modified version of this measure passed into law under the Conservatives as the County Councils Act in 1888. It provided for elected councils covering every ancient county, and the creation of the administrative county of London to replace the discredited Metropolitan Board of Works. The new county councils were made responsible for the upkeep of main roads in addition to the range of functions covered by their municipal counterparts.

In 1889, Gladstone censured Salisbury's government for not establishing district councils within the new county areas, and five years later he was able during his last ministry to rectify the omission with the Parish and District Councils Act.[51] Redlich and Hirst describe this as 'the last of the great constructive measures which built up a democratic system of local government in England'.[52] It pressed democratic consistency to its ultimate territorial limit by giving every village of 300 people or more its own elected council or parish meeting, while at district level the rural and urban sanitary authorities of 1875 became Urban and Rural District Councils elected on the same ratepaying franchise as the parish councils.

In the year after Victoria's death, the major councils assumed the role of Local Education Authorities as the School Boards, established under Forster's Education Act of 1870, were disbanded. Thus by the beginning of the 20th century the pattern of local government in England closely resembled its modern form.

The conflict between centralisation and local autonomy was never resolved to the entire satisfaction of either side. By establishing a tiered structure of local government, democratically elected at each level, parliament showed its faith in the principle of local autonomy over local affairs, but it retained control over all expenditure that necessitated borrowing on the security of the rates, so that in effect the last word was always with Westminster. Moreover, the progressive expansion of central government subsidies to local authorities meant a gradual diminution of effective independence. The Treasury through its grant system increasingly paid the piper and called the tune.

It is often assumed in discussing the merits of centralised control over local affairs, that progress invariably depended on initiative from the centre, that the authorities in London were for ever prodding provincial laggards into action, and that administrative reformers like Chadwick were constantly fighting the parochial parsimony and myopia of local opinion. The history of Leicester in the 19th century demonstrates that this was by no means always the case; not infrequently the town was in advance of the current philosophy at Westminster.

The men who served Leicester during the reign of Victoria were not always enlightened champions of municipal progress, but they invariably recognised the problems of the town and sought to tackle them with energy and determination. Occasionally their efforts led them into uncharted territory where others, including the central government, were to follow. It was above all in responding to the problems of health and housing that the local authorities in Leicester displayed imagination and initiative, and it is with its achievements in these and related fields that this book is primarily concerned. Let us first, however, introduce the town itself, the life in its streets, and the livelihood of its people, before looking more closely at its record in matters of health and housing.

Chapter One

THE LEICESTER SCENE

MOST VISITORS to Leicester are struck by its lack of distinction. Some, indeed, would agree with Thomas Baskerville, who described it in the late 17th century as 'an old stinking town situated upon a dull river'.[1] Those predisposed by long intimacy in its favour, make extravagant claims on its behalf. Leicester is, they assert, the seat of the legendary kingdom of Lear. It lies almost equidistant from Hadrian's wall and the English Channel, and is as far from Liverpool and Bristol as it is from Hull or Colchester, so that it stands in the middle of the English Midlands. One former mayor of Leicester was known to boast, therefore, that his town 'was historically, geographically and morally the centre of the British Empire'.[2] Its 'moral' entitlement to such a claim is, of course, even more dubious than the assumption of historical centrality, resting as it does on its nominal association with Simon de Montfort, Earl of Leicester, and putative father of the Mother of Parliaments.

If we were asked wherein lies the charm of Leicester, it would be its very lack of size and grandeur that would come to mind for it remains essentially a market town that can be seen and comprehended as a whole. One reason for this is the compact pattern of its principal thoroughfares, built over the lines of Roman streets and town walls. These walls, breached in the Civil War, became a readily accessible quarry for local builders and have disappeared almost entirely, but their course is clearly marked in the present street pattern by the ways which once lay alongside them: Soar Lane and Sanvey Gate to the north, with Church Gate and Gallowtree Gate to the east. The southern wall abutted for many years on to the fields used by horse traders and is known today as Horsefair Street. Within this rectangle bounded on the west by the river Soar, lies the old town, and when Susannah Watts wrote her account of a walk through Leicester in April 1804,[3] the town scarcely extended beyond the line of its ancient walls. Its population according to the census in 1801 was about 17,000. Only to the north-east, between Humberstone Gate and the canal, was there any appreciable growth. The Leicester Navigation which brought coal down from the Derbyshire pits brought also a great increase in warehouses, factories and homes stretching out from the town towards the canal wharf. By the accession of Victoria this segment of the town had become known as 'New Leicester', a suburb threatening to house as many as the town itself.

There was in this quarter the occasional building of architectural taste such as Spa Place, a relic of an abortive attempt to create a health resort from chalybeate springs on the site. The warehouses, inns, and dwellings fronting the wide roadway that extended from the Eastgates to Wharf Street were generally handsome structures befitting the prosperity of the merchants who traded here. But behind these to the north were the close-packed quarters of the urban proletariat. Here were row after row of mean tenements; and in some streets where older property lent itself to multiple occupation, there were the rookeries or lodging houses, the resort of itinerant Irishmen and others in search of a living.

Within the old town there were already some pockets of equally squalid housing, but for the most part Leicester remained a town of comparatively low density right through the 19th century.

This relative spaciousness of Leicester derived in part from its heritage as a large medieval borough which suffered a decline in the later Middle Ages, so that much of the land within the old walled area remained as gardens and orchards until the early 19th century. William Gardiner, a hosier and man of letters, who published a biographical work entitled 'Music and Friends', looked back on the town as he knew it in his youth and recalled that 'these tracts were enclosed in

Fig. 2. Leicester in 1828

every direction by walls made of mud and straw, forming dark and gloomy lanes', and he recalls his frightful sensation as a boy when 'passing through these dismal purlieus' in an evening.[4]

Eighteenth-century maps of Leicester show an abundance of trees within the town, an impression confirmed by Gardiner. He recalled especially the 'Pigeon Tree' in the Market Place, where the country women sat to sell pigeons, 'a great article of food brought from the open corn fields that surrounded Leicester in all directions'. There was also on the corner of Rutland Street a horse pond, where the porters from the local inns washed their horses. But, says Gardiner in 1853, 'All these rural features have disappeared. As our manufacturers and population have increased, the ground has become too valuable to allow these sylvan ornaments to remain'.[5]

Had Gardiner been writing of Nottingham or Coventry, he would have had even more cause to lament the passing of 'sylvan ornaments', for in both these places expansion was limited by the ancient rights of pasturage on the neighbouring opening fields exercised by the freemen.[6] Until these rights were limited by Act of Parliament builders had to compete for the diminishing space available within the existing built-up area. The land adjoining the borough of Leicester was markedly free from such restrictions. The east field had been enclosed in 1764 and thus made available for development, while the freemen had officially relinquished their holding in the south fields in 1804 in return for the provision of a smaller area of land to the west of the Welford Road which became known as Freeman's Common. The Corporation was therefore able to sell off some of its land in the former south fields as building plots, and to use some for other purposes such as the siting of the new cemetery in 1849. To the west of the river Soar very little building took place till the 1860s. This was in part due to the presence of two large private estates in the vicinity; the ancient manor of Westcotes, not demolished till 1866, and the estate known from the name of its 18th-century inhabitants as Danett's Hall. Susannah Watts, who lived at the Hall, described the pleasant walks through the cool shady scenery of this neighbourhood enjoyed by the citizens of Leicester in 1802.[7] When the last occupant of Danett's Hall, Dr. Noble, a prominent member of the reformed Corporation, died in 1861, the estate was sold for housing development.

To the north of the town lay one of the few large areas of open space upon which the townsfolk could walk and recreate themselves. This was St. Margaret's pasture (19 acres) on the east bank of the Soar, and adjoining it to the north-east was the land known as Abbey Meadow, very low and liable to flood. It was eventually purchased by the Corporation and laid out as a public park.

There was then no time in the 19th century when builders were unable to secure land upon which to extend the physical limits of the town, and the tendency toward concentration within the confines of the ancient borough was therefore much less than it would otherwise have been.

The standard of housing depends, however, not so much on the availability of land as on the rent that men can be expected to pay, and in Leicester the level of wages left precious little to spare. The rewards of framework knitting in the hosiery trade, which was the town's major industry, fell sharply in the years after the Napoleonic war; partly on account of a change of fashion which allowed mass-produced 'cut-ups', inferior imported hose cut from the cloth and seamed together, to compete with the traditional shaped stockings. Wages fluctuated around eight shillings a week in the three decades before 1850, and Thomas Cooper, the Leicester Chartist, was told that the stockingers of 1842 might earn no more than four shillings and sixpence.[8]

So bad was the situation among framework knitters that the government appointed a special Select Committee on the industry in 1844.[9] It was an easy trade to enter, requiring little skill and no capital, for the framework knitter could always hire a frame on which to work. The prevalence of this system led to the collection of frame rent even when stockingmakers owned their own machines, for in times of depression, the hosier supplying yarn would tend to favour those who were paying rent for their own frames, so that even independent stockingers found themselves obliged to pay the equivalent of 'frame rent' if they hoped to obtain yarn.

The troubles of the hosiery trade would have mattered less to the town if it had been one among several trades, but before the mid-century it was almost alone as the major employment of the time. No other industry came near to offering work on the same scale, so that bad years in the stocking trade meant bad years for the whole community.

The displacement of hosiery from this dominating position, as boot and shoe manufacture, engineering and other industries developed in the town help to explain the sudden rise in population which occurred in the 1860s. The decennial increase for 1851 to 1861 was only 12.3 per cent., barely enough to account for natural increase apart from any immigration.[10] The 1860s on the other hand showed an unparalleled growth of nearly 40 per cent., the highest recorded among the 20 largest towns in that decade and one that can only be explained in terms of immigration from outside the town.

Just why Leicester should have been so unattractive to the footloose in the previous decade is hard to explain. The forties, hungry or otherwise, were marked by two periods of outstanding depression culminating in the Chartist agitation of 1842 and 1848, yet the population of Leicester rose by a quarter in that decade. In the country as a whole the year of the Great Exhibition seemed to herald the onset of Victorian prosperity with a confidence and commercial success to which the Crimean war offered but a temporary and partial resistance. Leicester's refusal to reflect this mood would appear to stem from the unsettled state of its one major industry.

The census returns indicate the declining dominance of hosiery in Leicester. In 1851 out of a total of 15,252, 4,188 men over the age of 20 worked in the hosiery trade. The next biggest employer of adult male labour was the shoe trade which occupied 804 men over 20 years of age. Worsted manufacture, itself linked to the stocking trade, employed a further 506.[11] By 1861 the hosiery trade still dominated the workforce of 17,064 males above 20 with a labour intake of 3,320. Boot and shoe manufacture now absorbed 1,362, and worsted another 516.[12] In the succeeding decade, however, the balance moved decidedly in favour of shoe manufacture–3,714 out of 23,692 were classed as shoemakers, while hosiery workers now numbered only 2,867, and worsted manufacturers only 261, just half the number 20 years earlier. As an employer of labour worsted manufacture was far exceeded by the elastic web trade with 878 adult males and by engineering with 308, apart from the 151 who were employed in the making of spinning and weaving machines.[13]

The annual reports of the Domestic Mission, compiled every year by Joseph Dare for the Unitarian Great Meeting, bear witness to the change in the economic climate of Leicester. Dare was a native of Hinckley, on the south-western border of the county; he came to Leicester at the behest of the Unitarians in 1846 and his work took him regularly into the courts and habitations of the poorest citizens. It was said of him that no man in Leicester knew half as much of the lives of the poor as he did.[14] In his annual reports he spoke of 1847 and 1848 as years of 'very great privation and suffering to the poor, principally caused by want of employment',[15] and in 1848 he noted 'a season of unparalleled distress. Food dear, employment at an end, and the weather often very severe, vast numbers suffered greatly; and many are now feeling the lamentable effects of exhaustion and privation in fever, decline, and other consequent maladies'.[16]

By 1849 the worst was over, and he was able to record that the benevolent hand of Providence had 'crowned the year with goodness'.[17] The year 1850 saw 'continued prosperity' which Dare regarded as the essential base upon which moral improvement rested: 'A cheap loaf is a good educator'.[18] But the year of the Great Exhibition was 'a period of great difficulty'. 'The unfulfilled prayer for "leave to toil" is followed by involuntary idleness,' wrote Dare, and he spoke of 'several of the more respectable operatives who have taken up the "beggar's trade" rather than be forced into the Union-house'.[19]

The year 1852 was likewise a year of 'partial and irregular though increasing employment' in which several of the staple branches afforded employment 'for only a few months in the year'.[20] Slight improvement continued into 1853 and Dare was able to record 'a time of unusual prosperity' when 'the working classes generally were never so well off'.[21] But in the following years the doleful saga continued. The whole of 1854 was a 'very trying one' when 'scarcity or partiality (*sic*) of employment, the high price of fuel and provisions—and the severity of the winter, occasioned great and continual distress especially among the respectable poor'.[22] In the following two years, Dare reports similar distress, and while he makes no specific comment on the economic climate of 1857, his next report is a continuation of the chronicle of woe. 'The past winter was one of the most trying and difficult that I have ever experienced. My door was literally besieged with clamorous suppliants', he wrote, blaming in part the indiscriminate giving of alms. 'As the winter wore on distress became very general', and he added that he knew of several families 'driven into the Union house by starvation'.[23]

A respite from the gloom came in 1859, and this continued into the following year, though 1860 was 'not quite so prosperous' with 'extensive failures' and fluctuating employment.[24] The testimony of Joseph Dare thus suggests a decade of almost unrelieved stress in the main industry of Leicester—enough to deter many a would-be immigrant from settling in the town, and offering a plausible explanation of the reduced rate of expansion in Leicester's population at this time.

The decade which followed was a complete contrast, with industry thriving and the rapid growth of housing to keep pace with additional inhabitants. The Superintendent Registrar in 1871 attributed the remarkable expansion of the town to the depression of Coventry and troubles in the shoe trade at Northampton. The problems of Coventry were largely the result of the Cobden Treaty of 1860 which let French ribbons into England free of duty, while British manufacturers faced tariff barriers both on the Continent and in the

U.S.A.[25] The census returns for Coventry show a decline in these years from 40,936 in 1861 to 37,670 in 1871; the same decade saw the phenomenal 40 per cent. increase in the population of Leicester.

While the Coventry weavers were largely at the mercy of events, it would seem to be trade union militancy in the long-established Northampton shoe trade that induced some manufacturers to establish themselves in Leicester.[26] In 1853 Thomas Crick had invented his process of riveting soles to uppers, thereby earning the sobriquet 'father of the Leicester shoe industry'.[27] The manufacture of elastic webbing for boots and gloves also grew rapidly in these years from a mere service industry to one in its own right. A similar growth, from dependence on the hosiery trade to fully fledged independent existence, came over the engineering trade. At one time engineering in Leicester meant the making of stocking frames, but in 1861 specialist works were established for sewing-machine manufacture and for the production of shoe machinery. The human cost of industrial change as one trade contracted and others advanced must be left to the imagination. Joseph Dare gives us a hint of the effects upon men caught by the impersonal forces of technological change and structural unemployment. 'Many workmen suffer greatly', he wrote in 1862, 'from clinging to callings that are becoming superseded'.[28]

From 1863 Dare sounds a note of buoyancy in his annual reports. 'The past year has been one of unusual prosperity', he wrote, adding with dismay that loose habits had accompanied the growing prosperity: 'With the increase of population, we are fast losing the character of a quiet inland town . . . Wine shops, cigar divans, casinos, and public house dancing-rooms, not to mention other more disreputable places, are springing up in all parts of the town, offering temptations to spend money without profit, and alluring the thoughtless to degradation and ruin'.[29]

Like many a visionary, Dare saw the spiritual dangers of material progress. But the progress was real nonetheless, and more than once in the following decade Dare spoke of the town's 'unexampled Prosperity'.[30] It still suffered periodic recessions with unemployment and bankruptcies, but it never again experienced the prolonged gloom that depression in the hosiery trade invariably brought when that was the sole industry of importance. When Thomas Cooper wrote his memoirs in 1872 he contrasted the town with its state when he first addressed Chartist meetings there in 1842: 'How different', he wrote, 'is the condition of Leicester now thirty years have gone! All who enter it for the first time are pleased with the air of thrift the town wears, and the moving population of the streets. I saw lounging groups of ragged men in my time'.[31] When Dare wrote his last report to the Domestic Mission in 1876 he echoed the confidence and optimism of Cooper: The increase of the town is almost fabulous', he wrote, 'the dwellings of the poor are of much better construction; no industrious, sober artizan need live in an inconvenient house, none are built now back to back, or without back doors or windows'.[32] Nor, he might have added, was the industrious artisan, sober or otherwise, obliged to eke out a living as a framework knitter for want of any alternative employment.

One of the earliest factors which aided expansion in the industries of the town was the opening of the Leicester and Swannington Railway in 1832. John Ellis, a farmer at Beaumont Leys, near Leicester, approached George Stephenson, who was then engaged in constructing the Liverpool and Manchester Railway.[33] Stephenson bluntly told Ellis that he had enough to do, but he sent his son, Robert, to engineer the line. Its opening in July 1832 meant cheaper fuel for manufacturers as well as reducing the cost of coal to domestic users.[34] The firm of Ellis and Everard owes its foundation to the carriage of coal and quarry stone on this line.[35]

John Ellis and his son, Edward Shipley Ellis, both became chairmen of the Midland Railway Company which absorbed the Leicester and Swannington line in 1846. Edward Shipley Ellis was also chairman of the Board of Guardians, chairman of the Waterworks Company, and a leading figure in almost every philanthropic venture in the town. When he died in

1877, Francis Hewitt of the *Leicester Chronicle* wrote that it was 'well-nigh impossible to mention any matter of local importance which has taken place within the last half century which does not bear some record of an Ellis'.[36]

The Ellises were Quakers, but it was the Unitarians who, in the mid-19th century, dominated the municipal arena. Above all it was the brothers John and William Biggs who put themselves to the forefront of radical politics, each serving as mayor three times and each going on to sit at Westminster. Their political dominance was exercised through the ward committees of the local Reform Society. With the aid of Lawrence Staines, the Society's local agent, the Biggs brothers were able to influence not only the composition of the Town Council but also the choice of the borough members of parliament.[37] The economic foundation of this political dominance lay in the hosiery trade. They were reputed to employ a twelfth of all the hosiery workers in the town and county, and to own nearly 1,000 frames.[38] William was the more verbose and ambitious of the brothers. He gloried in his wealth and yearned to make his mark upon the fabric no less than the government of the town, boasting that he would, like Caesar, 'find it brick and leave it marble'. Others, like Thomas Corah, were more content to devote their energies to business.

It was Corah who in the late fifties imported some of Hine and Mundella's steam-powered rotary frames from Nottingham for use in his Leicester factory. His policy seems to have been to establish his ascendancy in the trade by gradually turning over his entire works to steam production before bringing his prices down to undersell his competitors like the Biggs brothers, who still depended on hand-powered machinery.[39] Corah's new works opened in 1866 near to the ancient Church of St. Margaret, which became the trade mark of the firm, now the oldest trade mark for knitted goods in use.[40] Corah's led the field also in the introduction of electric lighting among Leicester firms, demonstrating the advantages of the arc lamp some 20 years before the Corporation established its own generators in 1904.[41]

Several other Leicester firms became household names by the end of the century. Goddard's plate powder was the brainchild of Joseph Goddard, a chemist, who appreciated that one result of Farraday's experiments with electro-plating would be the supercession of mercurial cleaning powders then in use, since these would wear away the thin coating of silver plate. He therefore developed a non-mercurial plate powder and gave samples of it to the travellers who visited his chemist's shop.[42] The plate powder business soon outgrew the chemist's shop and became by degrees a giant concern for the manufacture of all kinds of wax and liquid polishes. It was Goddard's son, who on the death of his father, forsook his original calling as an architect, apprenticed to Sir George Gilbert Scott, and developed the business into a thriving international concern. So successful was he, that he was able to loan money to many other businesses in the early stages of growth; among them were the Bentley Engineering Group and Imperial Typewriters.[43]

Goddard was a Baptist like Thomas Cook, the Leicester pioneer of chartered trains and package tours. Cook, however, owed his initial success not to the repercussions of scientific experiment, but to the spread of teetolalism. Like most industrial towns Leicester was the scene of fervent activity by the Total Abstinence Union in the 1830s.[44] By 1840 Thomas Cook was engaged in the production of temperance propaganda and in the following year he conceived the idea of hiring a train to take a party of 500 teetotallers to a temperance rally in Loughborough Park. The excursion, which took place on Monday, 5 July 1841, proved to be the first of the endless succession of Cook's tours.[45] His success lay partly in his precise stipulation of terms and content of the tours. He published a book to accompany each of them, pointing out places of interest and giving all other necessary information. When the Great Exhibition came, he organised excursions to the Crystal Palace from all over the country; an estimated 165,000 visitors benefited from these arrangements.[46]

Cook had begun life as a gardener before he created his travel agency, graduating to the latter through furniture making, preaching and printing. Another man to begin in a very different calling from that with which he became chiefly associated, was William Kendall. He was a hairdresser who evidently resented the spoiling of his labours by the vagaries of the English climate. By the 1880s his sideline of umbrella-making became a thriving concern and he was moved to boast his talents in the following piece of doggerel:

We live in Leicester all our days,
  But very little know
Of manufactures carried on
  Without a deal of show.
We umbrellas carry too,
  The sun and storm to shade;
And yet it ne'er occurs to us
  To ask where they are made.

The factory in Northampton Street,
  O'er which Kendall is the boss,
Is the place where every one's produced
  That's really worth a toss.
They're made there for his retail trade,
  With light substantial frames,
And choicest sticks and fabrics rich,
  For gentlemen or dames.[47]

It was light industries of this sort which were to expand and multiply in the last decade of the 19th century and many such industries took root in Leicester where light engineering skill and a dexterous labour force already existed. Very little heavy industry was carried on in Leicester—the absence of a near source of iron being one obvious reason.

A few foundries were, however, established in Leicester, that of James Cort as early as 1799 beside the canal on a site next to St. Mark's Church, still known as Foundry Square. Goodwin Barsby, makers of specialist rock-crushing machinery, began their business in 1871 with a capital of £250. They later enlarged this meagre financial base by taking into partnership a wealthy ironmonger, Robert Pochin.[48]

The largest of the engineering firms in Leicester, that of Josiah and Benjamin Gimson, was founded in 1842, the Gimson brothers having served their apprenticeship at Cort's foundry. By 1878 Josiah was able to open his vast new Vulcan Works, adjoining the Midland Railway to the east of the town.[49] Josiah Gimson was the principal advocate of the Secular movement in Leicester. He and his family were nurtured in the rationalism of the Unitarian Great Meeting, but Josiah and his son, Sydney, pressed their doubts even beyond the broad limits of men like Joseph Dare. It was partly the intolerance of the Baptist committee of the Temperance Hall, built by Thomas Cook, in not allowing a platform to free thought that led Gimson and others to establish the Secular Hall in 1881.[50]

The building in Humberstone Gate, designed by the Derby architect, Larner Sugden, was something of a scandal to the Christian community, for it bears the bust of Jesus in evident equality of status with those of Voltaire, Tom Paine, Socrates and Robert Owen. It was opened in the presence of George Bernard Shaw, Charles Bradlaugh, and other prominent humanists, and became a sort of cathedral of unbelief, a place where all manner of social and political theorists found a congenial home.

Sydney Gimson, President of the Secular Society from 1888 to 1939, recalled how the minister of the Great Meeting often attended its functions. Having on one occasion listened to William Morris expound his view of the ideal society, the minister, the Rev. John Page Hopps, told him: 'You know Mr. Morris, that would be a very charming society that you have been describing, but it's quite impossible. It would need God Almighty to manage it!'. At this William Morris leapt to his feet, shook his fist in the parson's face and shouted: 'All right, man, you catch your God Almighty, we'll have him!'.[51]

Such audacious avowal of atheism, however, never gained widespread support in Leicester. The town was indeed remarkably devout in religious observance, as the census of 1851 demonstrated.

The Religious Census held on 30 March 1851 has been criticised as unreliable from the time it was conducted.

Nevertheless, its findings present virtually the only objective survey of the strength of different denominations in the reign of Victoria. The most marked feature of the pattern revealed for Leicester was the high overall level of church attendance at 62 per cent., far above the average of 49.7 per cent. for towns of over 10,000 population. Birmingham, by contrast, recorded only 36 per cent., Manchester 34 per cent., and London and its boroughs 37 per cent.[52]

Of the total of 10.4 million attending at all three services in England and Wales the Church of England and nonconformist churches claimed 47 per cent. each. Among the nonconformists, the Methodists represented about half the total, and the Baptists just under a fifth. But in Leicester these proportions were almost reversed. Taking figures from the best attended service, we find that 40.6 per cent. attended the Church of England; 38.3 per cent. went to Baptist or Independent services, and 17.3 per cent. were accounted for by the various Methodist churches of the borough, while 3.76 per cent. attended the Roman Catholic church. Despite their great influence on political affairs in the town, the Unitarians represented only 2.1 per cent. of the churchgoing populace and the Society of Friends less than half of one per cent.[53]

The extraordinary strength of the Baptists in Leicester is probably a reflection of the continuing influence of a number of outstanding individuals, among them, William Carey, the great missionary to India, Robert Hall, whose eloquence and intellect inspired admiration and respect far beyond his own congregation, and James Phillipo Mursell, a staunch supporter of the radical cause who entered with enthusiasm into the political battles of his day.

The Church of England had its dynamic leaders also: Canon David Vaughan, whose good work among the people of Leicester was almost legendary in his own time, and Canon John Fry, a passionate advocate of educational progress who was instrumental in founding the Church of St. John the Divine in Albion Street to minister to the needs of one of the poorest quarters of the town. Canon Fry later saw to the establishment of three other churches in predominantly working-class districts.[54]

But the churches with the most direct appeal to the poor were not those that sought to bring nearer the Kingdom of God on Earth, but those that promised, with less fear of refutation by self-evident reality, to satisfy the craving of the underdog for ultimate justice and reward. Hot gospelling of this sort flourished in the poorer districts of the town where such sects as the Mormons and the Fire Brigade of Jesus focussed their attention.[55]

Occasionally, evangelism and social concern went together, as in the ministry of the Rev. F. B. Meyer who came to Victoria Road Church in 1874. His unconventional approach and fervent evangelism led him to break away from the Baptist establishment in 1878, and to carry on his work at a mission in Infirmary Square. By 1881 his supporters had gathered sufficient funds to begin a church specifically built to hold Meyer in Leicester, Melbourne Hall. Here he was able to work among the poor and win hundreds of converts through the power of his preaching and the force of his example. He left Leicester in 1888 for Regents Park Church in London and became President of the Free Church Federal Council in 1904.[56]

Melbourne Hall remains to this day a citadel of evangelicalism; its plain red brick standing solidly among the dreary tenements of Highfields, a late Victorian suburb. It is a visible expression of the Calvinist rejection of outward grace, yet redeemed perhaps by its bleak and massive simplicity, contrasting strongly with the fussy facade of the Secular Hall which was built in the same year.

Few of Leicester's buildings would strike us today as architecturally noteworthy. We tend rather to condemn the vandalism which led Victorian developers to demolish medieval buildings like the timber-framed chapel of St. Ursula's in Wyggeston's Hospital and the old *Blue Boar* inn, where Richard III spent his last night before Bosworth. To contemporaries it was a source of pride that timbered houses and Georgian stucco made way for brick structures of more 'refined' taste.

The high Tory, Robert Read junior, regarded the Victorian clock tower as a 'thing of beauty' and 'a joy for ever', while he castigated the rebuilt Corn Exchange and its 'hideous bridge of sighs' as unworthy of the market place.[57] Councillor F. T. Mott, a wine merchant with a penchant for culture and the assurance that only the complete amateur can afford, fastened on the advent of the gable as the turning point from vulgarity to refinement in the Victorian town. The 'straight unbroken cornice has disappeared from the skyline',[58] he declared, and enthused over the variety of gabled roofs that had mushroomed in its place. In Mott's eye, the stuccoed Temperance Hall was 'a ponderous sham' and the Market Hall 'a monster'. He denounced the plastered brickwork of neo-classical buildings as 'pretending to be stone, but with none of the beautiful texture, or rich tints, or durability' of the real thing, and he praised instead the gabled grandeur of contemporary architecture. 'The new churches and chapels, the Wyggeston and Board schools, the Town Hall, the villa residences, the Hospitals, the blocks of offices, and some of the present shops, have scattered over our town an immense amount of true, honest, beautiful art, which is daily doing its good work in educating the popular taste and making the life of the people brighter, happier and healthier'.[59]

Such exuberance was widely shared, for this was the Leicester that contemporary opinion liked to see. There was an uglier, poorer side, of squalid overcrowded houses in confined courtyards; of men and women working 12 or 14 hours a day in backyard workshops; of drunkenness and hopeless poverty. But the dominant impression made by Victorian Leicester is one of decided advance and change for the better. The town motto, 'Semper eadem', was never less appropriate than in the reign of Victoria.

Chapter Two

THE REFORMED CORPORATION

THE STRENGTH of radicalism in Leicester during the 19th century was, to a very large extent, a reaction against the corrupt Tory administration that preceded the reform of municipal corporations in 1835. If the 'wicked old body' had sinned less blatantly, the Conservatives would have stood a far better chance of regaining popular support. As it was, however, they were never able to shake off the legacy of the unreformed Corporation, and it was over 100 years before they again commanded a majority in the council chamber.

The intensity of this reaction can only be understood if we look at the record of the unreformed Corporation in its last years. It was a self-electing body chosen out of the ranks of the freemen. No dissenter or Whig was invited to participate in its deliberations. They were not appointed to any offices under the Corporation, nor did they benefit from the various charitable funds at its disposal. Moreover, since voting in general elections was the privilege of freemen, and only the Corporation could confer the freedom of the borough, the choice of Leicester's parliamentary representatives was virtually the prerogative of the Corporation. An influential minority of the town's leading citizens thus found itself effectively disfranchised and excluded from any say in the government of the town.

When the Webbs compiled their mammoth work on English local government they recorded their view that Leicester stood out in the 18th century as the town in which there was 'least mention of public improvements of any kind'.[1] They quote a resolution passed at a public meeting in 1822 which declared 'that the streets of the town were in a state of uncleanliness, filth, and neglect, repugnant to every feeling of decency, destructive of the comfort and injurious to the health of the inhabitants'.[2] The record of the old Corporation was not in fact so black as its radical critics implied, for in that same year, the Corporation proposed to obtain a parliamentary Bill to pave, sewer and light the streets of the town. The Bill was dropped through the opposition of the ratepayers, partly on account of the added power that such a measure might put into the hands of the ruling oligarchy.[3] Reform was thus strangled by the political fears of the reformers themselves. No doubt these fears were justified, for as the Webbs put it, 'the members of the Corporation never scrupled to use their whole influence and authority, whether as magistrates, as landlords, as trustees of charities, or as Municipal administrators, to put their own party in power'.[4] They quote the Commissioners Inquiring into Municipal Corporations in 1835, who declared that: 'From the Mayor to the humblest servant of the Corporation, every office has been filled by members of the Corporation, or so called Tory party, to the total exclusion of all who entertained different opinions, however wealthy, however intelligent, however respectable'.[5]

Despite its pervasive influence, the Corporation was not able to dictate how existing freemen would vote; and in 1818 it suffered a substantial rebuff in the election of Thomas Pares, as one of the M.P.s for the borough. This was the first time that the official Corporation candidate failed to be elected, and the Tory establishment of the borough under the guidance of the Town Clerk, Thomas Burbidge, fought back strenuously to regain the seat in 1826. Elections were generally expensive affairs especially if the franchise was widely held as in Leicester, where 4,781 freemen went to the polls in that year.[6] Beer and bribery were the normal means by which votes were won, but in addition the Corporation sought to increase its share of the votes by the simple expedient of creating new honorary freemen on an unprecedented scale as 1826 approached.

The election itself was closely fought and resulted in the success of the two Tory candidates, Charles Abney Hastings and Robert Otway Cave. There, however, the victory of the Corporation ended, for an unseemly squabble soon arose over the payment of Cave's election expenses. Cave thereupon became so opposed to his former supporters that he not only voted for Catholic Emancipation, but became the spokesman for Leicester Liberals favouring the repeal of the Test and Corporation Acts, which kept nonconformists out of public office. The exact extent of the debts incurred by the borough on Cave's behalf is difficult to determine, but his friends asserted that the total Tory outlay was about £40,000.[7]

Deprived of Cave's payments for services rendered, the Corporation plunged itself deeper in debt by mortgaging its estates to the Rev. Henry Palmer of Carlton Curlieu for £10,000 at an interest of 4 per cent.[8]

Such mishandling of corporate funds made admirable sport for the eager young barristers who visited Leicester in 1834 as commissioners inquiring into the government of municipal corporations. Their report, drawn up with the support of prominent radicals in the town and in the face of the implacable opposition of Thomas Burbidge, the Town Clerk, was a damning indictment of political jobbery and misappropriation of funds. It showed not only the use of corporate funds in order to influence the outcome of elections, but also peculation in regard to the sale of the former south fields. One of the chief beneficiaries was Thomas Burbidge himself.[9]

When it became clear that reform was imminent, the old Corporation urgently petitioned the House of Lords against the Municipal Corporations Bill, Burbidge taking a prominent part among the town clerks who travelled to Westminster to give evidence against the Bill. Finally, when the Bill became law, the Tory councillors proceeded to sell off Corporation property as if it belonged to them personally. They granted life pensions to various officers of the Corporation and presented substantial pieces of plate to the value of 450 guineas to the town clerk and two of the aldermen who had exerted themselves in the fight against the Bill.[10] In fact, the effrontery of this last distribution of spoils so damaged the cause of the Tory candidates that Burbidge and the two aldermen returned their gifts the next day.[11] The damage, however, was done.

The Conservative *Leicester Journal*, sensing the impending doom of the old regime, urged its readers on the eve of the election 'to devote their whole energies of mind and body to the cause of the Constitution' [12] Significantly its criticism of the reform candidates as 'men who themselves never knew the properties of a straight line' were coupled with an attempt to dissociate the Tories from the discredited system: 'The Conservative candidates have no more to do with the old corporation than with a company of dancing Dervishes!'[13] But the *Journal's* warnings of the 'immediate and ultimate results of Socinian ascendancy' to wit, 'the speedy destruction of the Church, and the eventual despotism of the sword',[14] went unheeded. Tory domination was replaced overnight by a Liberal control which was almost as complete. 'Would that we might consign to eternal oblivion the events of the past week!' cried the anguished editor of the *Journal* after the election.[15]

In no other town was the transfer of power so total and long-lasting. In Nottingham the Liberals were already in control before 1835; in towns like Southampton and Exeter the Conservatives maintained control, while in some of the northern industrial towns like Leeds reaction against higher rates led to the defeat of reformist Liberal administrations within the space of a few years. [16]

The Whig and radical alliance in Leicester gained 38 of the 42 seats on the new Council and, of the remainder, two were accorded to the Conservatives only by the casting vote of the retiring mayor. To these new councillors were added a further 14 reforming aldermen, making 56 members on the new Corporation. The affinity between nonconformity and radicalism is indicated by the analysis of religious affiliations on the new body. The hub of political power centred upon the 12 members from the Unitarian Great Meeting which provided the first seven mayors of the reformed Corporation, and so became known as the 'Mayors' Nest'. Numerically the Unitarians were outnumbered by

16 Anglicans, equalled by the 12 Baptists and nearly so by the 10 Independents, but their influence as a sect was out of all proportion to their numbers as was that of the Quakers who had three council members in 1836. By contrast the Wesleyans, still in their apolitical stage, numbered only two members.[17]

This connection between political radicalism and nonconformity evolved partly as a result of the exclusion of dissenters from office under the Test Acts which were not repealed till 1828, and partly from the accumulated resentment of nonconformists against the Tory Corporation which was blatantly hostile towards dissent.

Until 1749 when a court case went in their favour, it had even been impossible for dissenters to set up in business within the borough. Such exclusiveness on the part of the Anglican Tory Corporation led to a polarisation of political and religious opinion. Radicals and nonconformists had been welded together in their effective disfranchisement and the centre of religious unorthodoxy, the Unitarian Great Meeting in Bond Street, had come to be the hub of political opposition to the Corporation.

The Unitarians were more committed to freedom of thought than any other dissenting sect. Theologically they represented the extreme left, 'the dissidence of Dissent'; they were not so much concerned with individual salvation as with the advancement of God's Kingdom on Earth, and political power was but one means to that end. The Great Meeting drew to itself therefore many of the town's most lively and enquiring minds. As the Tory historian, Throsby, remarked in 1791, 'the congregation is genteel and numerous; several of the first families of the town are of this sect'.[18] The banking wealth of the Pagets, the industry and legal ability of Samuel Stone, the hosiery fortune of the Biggs family, the nascent engineering skill of the Gimsons, and the solid business interests of wool and worsted spinners like Fielding Johnson, Coltman, Brewin and Whetstone were all to be found within its doors.

It has been stated that the members of the new Council in 1836 differed little in occupational and social status from their predecessors,[19] but while it is true that 'hosiers were well represented in both bodies' and retailers appeared on both, there was a marginal shift toward the representation of larger business interests and somewhat fewer shopkeepers on the new council. (See Tables on pp. 166-7.) The representation of bankers, gentlemen and the medical profession was also marginally stronger in 1836 than in 1835. The new men were, in general, champions of frugality and honesty in the affairs of the town. Their rejection of civic pomp and extravagance was typified in the decision to sell off the Corporation mace and plate. The entire collection of two civic maces, town plate and regalia was sold with a Cromwellian disdain for baubles.[20]

Every action of the Corporation came under the same scrupulous eye to the saving of money and avoidance of waste. The new Town Clerk was Samuel Stone, another Unitarian, who had taken a prominent part in the Liberal opposition to the unreformed Corporation. Stone's methodical thoroughness eventually led him to compile his famous *Justices' Manual* and other works of reference for the legal profession. His formal and impersonal letters as Clerk are filed neatly for all the 36 years of his tenure of office. Rarely does the man emerge from behind the official mask, but his partner, Paget, gives an inkling of the mentality of the new regime when, during Stone's indisposition with chickenpox in 1837, he told a London firm that their bill for services rendered would 'have to undergo the ordeal of a Reform Town Council' and he added, 'you don't know what they are in London, but we who live in a Corporate Town are fully alive to its scrutinising eyes'.[21]

Old servants of the Corporation found themselves suddenly without their regular income. The new Council refused in sympathetic terms to continue the trivial payment of £10 each to Miss Valentine and her sister as town organists,[22] but summarily dismissed Thomas Yates as Coroner and superintendent of the cattle market. The Council maintained that it was not obliged to pay any compensation because his appointment was 'during pleasure' only and not for life. Yates claimed compensation for loss of office under the Municipal Corporations Act. His claim was not upheld, although seven other servants of the old Corporation were granted compensation by the new Council, some continuing to receive payment for the next 20 years.

There was, however, justifiable reluctance to reward further those who had been the principal beneficiaries of graft and corruption under the old regime. The chief loser by the Reform Act had been Thomas Burbidge, the ex-Town Clerk, and his claim for loss of office amounted to a considerable sum of money. Burbidge in fact claimed £13,000 in loss of earnings and he seems to have been fairly confident of receiving this, for in October 1837 he wrote to Stone privately asking if he could procure a loan of £400 to £500 'on my compensation account'.[24] Burbidge was in acute financial difficulties at the time, not having the money to pay his rent to Lord Stanford, and was driven to ask Stone for this personal favour.

The magnitude of Burbidge's effrontery staggered his opponents. Burbidge had drawn into his own hands almost every office of profit under the old Corporation, had sold lands to himself at advantageous prices, and repeatedly refused to deliver up the account books of the Corporation either to the Parliamentary Commissioners or to his own successor. He misappropriated the funds of both Sir Thomas White's charity and the Wyggeston's Hospital and was exceedingly lucky to have escaped criminal charges on all these counts. Yet when dismissed from his post as Clerk to the Corporation, he had the temerity to claim compensation and to seek a personal loan on the strength of his entitlement to such redress.

Burbidge's claim hung heavily upon the new Corporation for many years. It was eventually settled in his favour in 1853 when the Corporation agreed to pay him £400 and £600 a year for the rest of his life. Fortunately for the ratepayers this terminated two years later in a debtors' jail, to which he had been consigned by his wine merchant for failure to pay his bills.[25]

Municipal reform was at this time almost synonymous with economising in expenditure from the rates. The new Council saw such economy as its primary duty and only gradually came to see its role in the provision of civic amenities as conflicting with this economy.

The Beginnings of Sanitary Reform

It was out of this conflict that the major political confrontation occurred within the new Liberal Corporation. The radicals pressed for civic improvements, while the more moderate Whiggish element stuck firmly to a belief in economy. E. P. Hennock has described this duel between the improvers and economists as it affected Birmingham and Leeds, where the broader vision of the wealthier Liberal interests was over-ridden by shortsighted parsimony among ratepayers and small shopkeepers.[26] In Birmingham the town clerk was removed from office, the surveyor replaced by an assistant at half his salary, and important schemes for improvement were delayed for years. In Leeds a similar reaction against large outlay from the rates led to a prolonged era of municipal impotence in the face of growing problems of sanitation and overcrowding. The wealthier and professional classes in both cities tended to opt out of political involvement and leave matters in the hands of petty traders, builders, landlords and others with scant regard for sanitary reform and a rooted aversion to high rates.[27]

In Leicester the conflict was never seen in quite the same terms. Improvers and economists were united in their desire for better civic amenities. They disagreed only in their order of priorities. Moreover, the split between improvers and economists was contained within the ranks of the Liberal party and it did not follow any marked economic cleavage of interest; wealthy manufacturers and professional men were to be found in both camps.

Amongst the most persistent and powerful advocates of financial retrenchment was Joseph Whetstone. His grandfather, also named Joseph, was one of the first to introduce Arkwright's roller principle into the worsted spinning trade in 1787.[28] The young Whetstone became a partner in the firm of Brewin and Whetstone and had an interest with John Ellis and others in the creation of the Leicester and

Swannington railway. When he died he was said to be the most extensive employer of labour in the district, with interests in two spinning mills, two coal mines, and brick and tile works.

Whetstone was the chief spokesman on financial matters in the reformed Corporation and a consistent advocate of caution and economy in the spending of public funds. It was he who chaired the Finance Committee appointed in 1836 to investigate the operations of the old Corporation. When, in his mayoral year, 1839–1840, it was proposed to obtain an Improvement Act to carry out a number of alterations, including the widening of the West Bridge, Whetstone expressed the reluctance of the Improvement Committee to incur the expense of an Act of Parliament. In view of 'the depressed state of trade, and the financial condition of the Borough' and 'whilst Mr. Burbidge's claim for so large a sum was undetermined, and the Charity Commissioners' suit against the Council for the large defalcation by Mr. Burbidge in Sir Thomas White's charity, remained unsettled' it would be 'highly injudicious and imprudent' to proceed with the proposed Bill.[29]

But if he resisted expenditure on superficial improvements, Whetstone never sought to economise on what he regarded as essential to the health of the community. From 1839 he had advocated an extension of sewerage and drainage and he was one of the earliest advocates of a municipal water supply. In this he was actuated partly by his interests as an industrialist. He wanted an improved water supply not only because it would enable him to conduct his dyeing business more efficiently, but because the premiums paid in fire insurance would be considerably less if an adequate water supply were available.[30]

Of the various suggested improvements contemplated in 1840, the most pressing was the reconstruction of the West Bridge, which straddled the river Soar in picturesque stone arches with a cluster of buildings close to its banks. It was inconvenient, unsafe, and a contributing cause of periodic flooding. The Council decided to proceed with this improvement in isolation as soon as the legal obstacles were overcome in November 1840. The remainder of the Bill was shelved in 1841 because of 'the depressed state of trade and the financial condition of the Borough'.[31]

By 1843 economic conditions had so far improved and the town's debts had been so much reduced that talk once more arose of carrying out the projected improvements. Public improvement, as the *Chronicle* said, was 'the order of the day', and Leicester, which had fallen behind other towns because of its 'laudable desire to get out of debt', was now able to follow the example of other large towns. Liverpool was about to spend £2½ million on assize courts, Manchester had embarked on the opening up of confined courtyards and the provision of parks; Edinburgh had its public baths, while 'Birmingham, Sheffield, Preston–and to come nearer home', said the *Leicester Chronicle,* 'even Ashby de la Zouch–are all actually on the stir, or about to be so, to add to public health, comfort and convenience, by arrangements for improving their streets, buildings or suburbs'.[32]

In the meantime, a powerful stimulus to improve the town's sewerage and drainage appeared in the publication of the Sanitary Report of 1842. Edwin Chadwick's Report on the Sanitary Condition of the Labouring Population was intended to shock the nation into action against the dangers of environmental pollution. The people of Leicester had every reason to heed its warning, for, although the town never exhibited the close-packed slums of Manchester and Liverpool in the early 1840s, its death rate almost equalled theirs, standing at 30 per 1,000. Chadwick's Report was reprinted in the *Leicester Chronicle,* where it was certainly read by a number of influential citizens. The editor of the *Chronicle* was James Thompson, a thorough-going advocate of the Liberal cause, a man of wide interests and outstanding ability. Apart from writing most of the leading articles for upwards of 30 years, Thompson wrote a number of historical works based largely on his own researches into the records of the borough of Leicester.[33] He was a founder member of the Leicester Archaeological Society, and sat as a Liberal councillor from 1867 to 1870. Although himself a Baptist, he was educated by the Rev. Charles Berry of the Unitarian

Great Meeting and came to know many of the town's leading figures as his personal friends. Throughout his life he remained a warm admirer of Joseph Whetstone.

It was probably partly from Thompson's printed extracts of Chadwick's Sanitary Report that Whetstone gained his conviction of the imperative need for sanitary reform. He had already in 1841 supported proposals for comprehensive sewerage and drainage works, and whenever the subject of town improvement was again raised Whetstone insisted that attention to these matters should take precedence over all others.

The Council appeared to endorse this view and Whetstone successfully carried a motion in 1845 calling for the adoption of a 'thorough and efficient system'[34] of drainage. The cry was echoed by Thompson in the *Leicester Chronicle*:

> Above all, let it not be forgotten, that though we can carry on our municipal affairs under the roof of the old Town Hall—can put up for a time with the inconveniences of a small market place and cattle markets in the thoroughfares—and can tolerate the existing deficiency of Post Office accommodation,—we cannot, we ought not, to rest satisfied for a day longer with a state of things which causes our townsmen to be afflicted with fevers, and which every year sweeps thousands of them into premature graves. If we do remain thus indifferent and content in our neglect of sanitary measures, at the same time knowing what the effects of our neglect are, our guilt is obvious and enormous. We may lull ourselves into criminal ease for a time, but a dark and heavy curse will ere long cast a broad shadow over our own selfish homes. Offended duty will not long remain unavenged.[35]

Despite such solemn warnings, however, William Biggs, who had just returned from America, proceeded to press upon the Council a measure of improvement in which sewerage and water supply were conspicuously absent.[36] The new Improvement Bill seemed to have as its chief object precisely those things which Joseph Whetstone and James Thompson regarded as less important. This division between the 'economists' and the 'improvers' threatened to erupt into open conflict within the Liberal ranks for the next 30 years.

William Biggs's brother, John, who had already twice been chosen as mayor, declared in the council chamber that he was tired of economy in the financial affairs of the borough and would in future advocate a more lavish spending of public funds. Civic pride demanded wider streets, parks, a new cemetery, an improved post office, and above all, something more commodious and convenient than the 14th-century Guildhall as the seat of town government. The ostensible reason for the absence of any reference to sewerage and water supply in the Bill presented by William Biggs was that these were to be provided by Chadwick's Towns Improvement Company which was then being canvassed.

The competence of any private company to install sewerage and supply water, even if the losses on the former were weighed against the profits of the latter, must surely have been problematical; and in fact Chadwick's Towns Improvement Company, to which Biggs alluded, collapsed in the following year, 1846.[37]

To Joseph Whetstone the new Improvement Bill was a complete reversal of his programme, putting the embellishment and adornment of the town before essential sanitary improvements. He opposed Biggs's measure in three successive Council meetings, and urged that nothing be done until the sewerage system had been attended to. The persistence of this rearguard action evidently needled William Biggs and there was a note of asperity in his formal motion of 1845 'that the decision of the Council upon this subject as evidenced by decisive majorities upon three occasions be respected, approved and confirmed'.[38] The voting was two to one against Whetstone, but he continued to press hostile amendments. His attitude was abundantly clear: 'he could never sanction by any act of his, an outlay of public money for purposes of ornament, before the health of the town had been provided for; and if this Council should determine on going ahead with this bill, before providing for the drainage of the town, he should certainly not take upon himself the responsibility of the financial business any longer'.[39]

Evidently this ultimatum from the most widely-respected member of the Council had the desired effect, for in the New Year a compromise was reached whereby the chief bone of contention—the new Town Hall—was dropped from the Bill and other reductions made in the plans of the Improvement Committee.[40]

As for the cemetery, there was general agreement as to the need for a comprehensive solution, but religious prejudice seemed a barrier to progress on non-denominational lines and a company was established instead to provide a separate cemetery for the nonconformist population of the town, as had been done at Nottingham in 1836.

Once again the Biggs brothers, as strong advocates of a denominational cemetery, found themselves in opposition to Joseph Whetstone, who insisted on a comprehensive measure embracing the Anglicans also. There was some criticism, too, of the private company for having obtained Corporation land at a price below its market value.[41] Charged with sectarianism and suspected of jobbery, the company promoters deferred to their critics and agreement was eventually reached with the Anglicans for a general cemetery; an Act for this purpose received the Royal Assent in May 1848.[42]

But still nothing had been done to promote 'the better drainage of the town' which had been a principal object of the abortive Bill of 1841. Despite the publicity given to the subject by Chadwick's report of 1842, and despite the repeated pleas of Whetstone and the *Leicester Chronicle*, the town remained insanitary and badly drained, whilst its population continued to rise.

In the wake of the Sanitary Report of 1842 and the revelations of the Health of Towns Commission which followed it, the Whig government of 1846 bestirred itself so far as to pass an Act for the Removal of Nuisances which aimed to facilitate the work of sanitary authorities. It empowered them to enforce the removal of filth from streets and of pigs from the neighbourhood of dwelling places, and to order that overflowing cesspits and other public nuisances be dealt with.[43]

Responsibility for enforcing this Act normally devolved on the local Boards of Guardians, but since in Leicester the Council had already assumed control over such nuisances as obstruction of the causeway, and since it had also appointed an Inspector of Nuisances, it was not surprising that the implementation of the Act of 1846 was regarded as the province of the Council rather than that of the Board of Guardians. The Inspector of Nuisances at the time was George Bown, a veteran radical who had been arrested for his Jacobin sympathies in 1794.[44] For a brief period in 1813, he edited the *Leicester Chronicle*, and when the Liberals came to power in 1835 he became Receiver of Flour Returns and Accountant to the Council. To the niggardly income he thus received was added £20 per annum in 1840 for his services as Inspector of Nuisances. The office had been created in 1836 at the suggestion of the Surveyors of Highways, who proposed that Frederick Goodyer, the newly-appointed Chief Constable, should report any public nuisances encountered by his men in the course of their duties. Bown succeeded as Inspector of Nuisances when Goodyer took up his more lucrative post as Chief of the County Police Force in 1839.[45]

George Bown went about the business of identifying risks to health as firmly convinced of the pythogenic theory as any of his contemporaries. When the state of the Soar was under discussion in 1850, he likened its polluted condition to the Pontine marshes. 'In the memory of persons now living', he wrote, 'these portions of the river were limpid and transparent streams, teeming with fish. In fact, they are now torpid and turbid, particularly the latter part, which has become an enormous open cesspool of every species of animal and vegetable refuse, in a constant state of decomposition—incessantly generating volumes of those pestiferous gasses which, even in a moderate degree of concentration, cause disease of the most malignant and mortal character'. Bown described how the 'pestilential malaria' arising from the polluted Soar 'spreads an invisible canopy of disease over our dwellings, penetrating into our parlours and bedrooms, and too often wrapping its victims in the shroud of death'.[46]

The Appointment of Medical Officers

When Bown reported to the Council on the sanitary state of the town in October 1846, it was therefore natural that he regarded all sources of atmospheric pollution as dangerous to health. Bown asserted that there was 'scarcely a court-yard, alley or narrow street, particularly in the lower parts of the town, that has not its accumulation of filth to an extent highly prejudicial and dangerous to its inhabitants and the neighbourhood'. Bown listed many specific examples of foul ditches and cesspools and observed that: 'In the more crowded parts of the town the frequent close contiguity of slaughter houses, pigsties and privies, the latter too with walls seldom more than three feet in height, are a perpetual source of visitation: the poisonous exhalations from which, having no chance of escape, even in brisk winds, the surrounding houses form a kind of cistern of concentrated contamination, never wholly dispersed, and which is not easy to dilute or dissipate'. All this, said Bown, was but 'a mere fraction of the accessible sources of mischief which prevail in abundance in every quarter of the town'.[47]

Together with his report he submitted three certificates, each duly signed by two medical practitioners certifying the existence of particular nuisances. At this point, Bown observed also that the Nuisances Removal Act might be brought into more effectual operation if the medical men could be rewarded for their services, since the inspection and certification of nuisances was a time-consuming and thankless task, not readily undertaken by professional men at their own expense.

Despite Bown's fears that such remuneration would not be legal, the Council decided forthwith to appoint two men as Medical Officers and to pay them a salary of 20 guineas per annum out of the Improvement Fund.[48] Dr. John Barclay, a spirited and energetic physician to the Royal Infirmary, and Mr. John Buck, a surgeon who was later to control the County Lunatic Asylum,[49] thus became in October 1846 the first medical officers appointed by a local authority in Britain.

1. View of Leicester in 1845

2. The old West Bridge

3. The West Bridge of 1841

4. The present West Bridge built in 1891

East Bond Street Unitarian Chapel, 'The Great Meeting', 1708, with porch added 866

6. The Crescent, King Street, *c*.1820

7. Spa Place, Humberstone Road, 1789

The Secular Hall, Humberstone Gate,
881, by Larner Sugden

9. Melbourne Hall in Melbourne Road, Highfields, 1881, by Goddard and Paget

10. The Corn Exchange in the Market Place, 1850, with its steps and upper storey ad
by F. W. Ordish in 1855; in front, statue of the Duke of Rutland, 1852

11. The Museum, New Walk, 1836, by J. A. Hansom

2. Thomas Cook's Temperance Hall in Granby Street, 1853, by James Medland

. Old Gas Works and lime kilns on the site of what is now Charles Keene College of rther Education

14. The old Town Hall or Guildhall dating from about 1350, from John Flower's drawing of 1826

15. The new Town Hall designed by F. J. Hames, opened in 1876

16. Samuel Stone

17. Joseph Whetstone

18. Cramant's Yard, King Street, as it is today

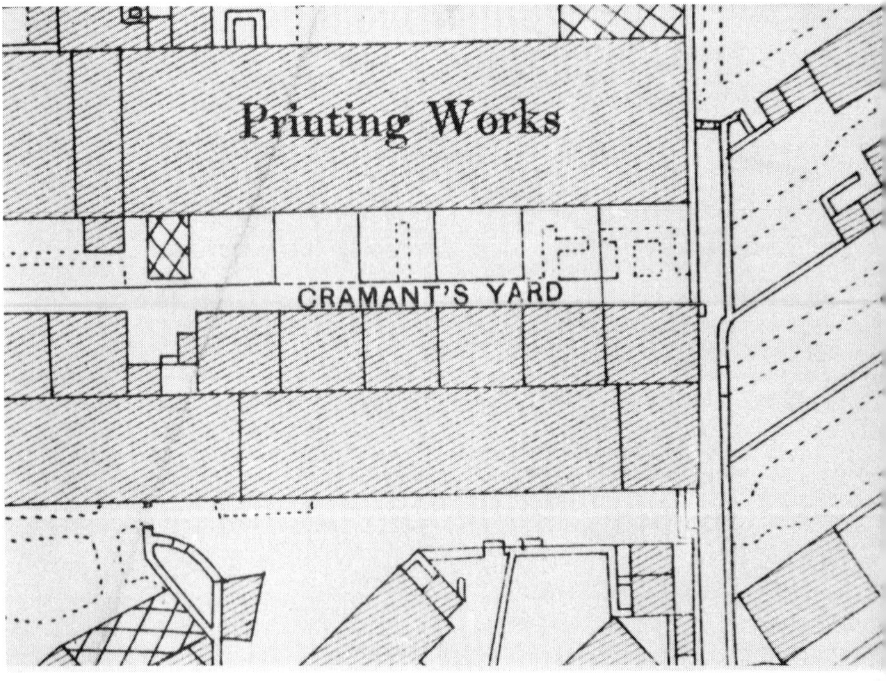

19. Cramant's Yard as shown on the O.S. map of 1885

20. A court off Burleys Lane, demolished in 1937

22. A court off Belgrave Gate, behind number 105, demolished in 1937

23. Dr. Noble talking to his gardener in the grounds of Danetts Hall

24. Housing to the rear of Dannett Street on the 7th estate of the Freehold Land Society

25. Curzon Cottages, typical of thos erected in compliance with the bye-la close to Thomas Bland's houses in Cu Street photographed in 1953 and den lished about ten years later

26. (*below*) The Victoria Model Loc House, Brittania Street, 1887, by Th Hind

7. Detail from the facade of the Victoria Model Lodging House showing national tereotypes of Welsh and English in carved brickwork

28. As in No. 27 (*above*), showing a Scot and an Irishman

29. Council housing in Winifred Street, 1900

30. (*overleaf*) The Clock Tower, 1868, by J. Goddard with the East Gates Coffee H
1885, by Edward Burgess, in the background

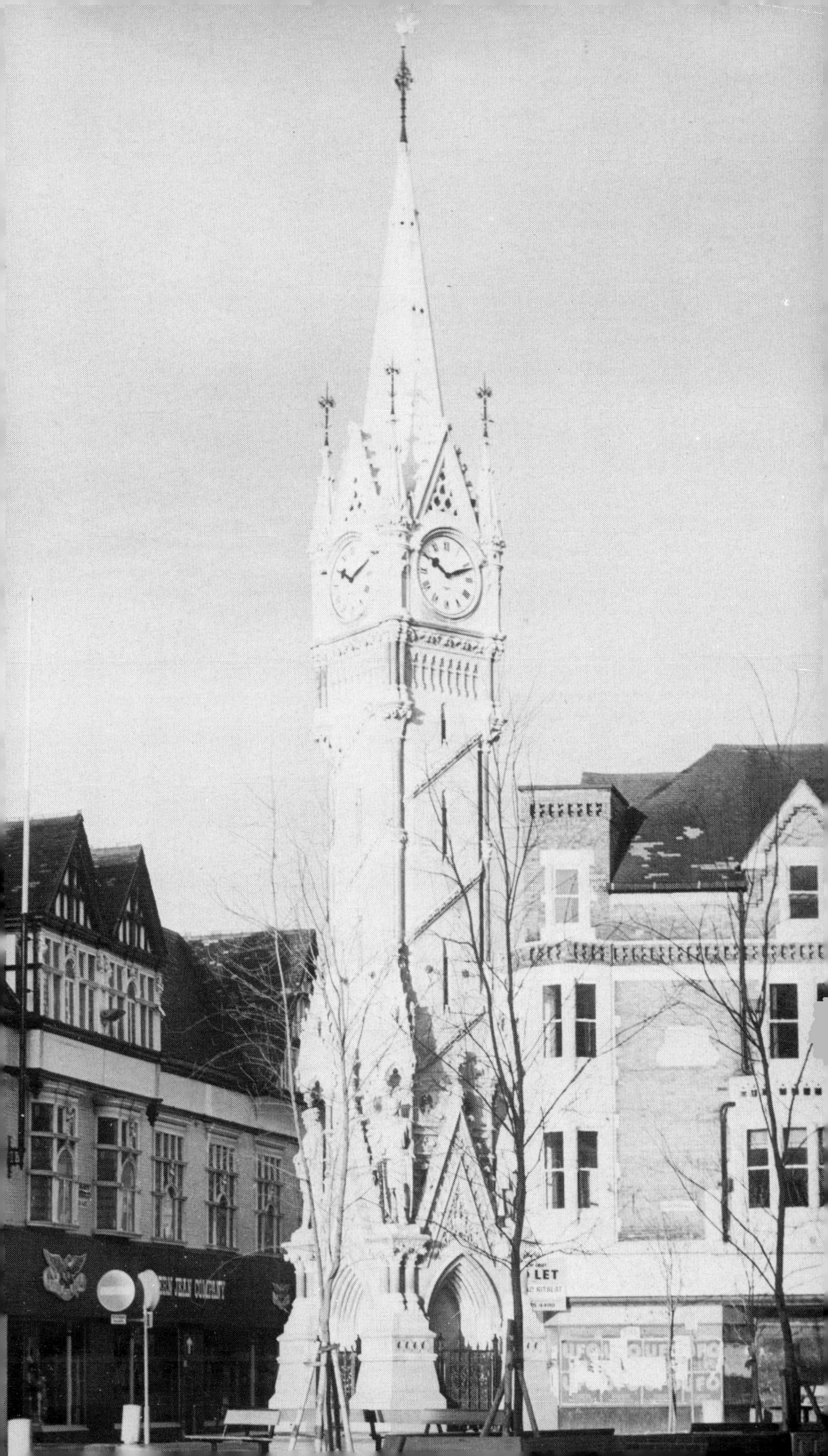
LET

31. The original pavilion in Abbey Park, 1881, by James Tait

32. A horse-drawn tram brought into service during the coronation celebrations in 1

33. The Cattle Market, Welford Road, 1872, J. B. Everard

34. The new Gas Works on Aylestone Road, 1878

35. High Cross Street as drawn by John Flower in the early nineteenth century

The High Cross re-erected in Cheapside in the north-eastern corner of the Market ce in 1976

37. John Biggs facing the modern civic centre with Samuel Stone's office in the background, designed by William Flint in 1842

The two men were not, it is true, designated Officers of Health, though this is in fact what they were, and they can lay claim to having filled the office three months before the appointment of W. H. Duncan in Liverpool. Duncan took up his duties in January 1847, under the Liverpool Improvement Act of the previous year, and a year later he was confirmed in his post as the first full-time Medical Officer of Health in the country.[50] Even so, his conception of his role at that time accords less with the way the office developed in later years than did that of Barclay and Buck in Leicester.

It is stated by Royston Lambert, biographer of Sir John Simon, that Duncan was 'content with the mere tabulation of statistics',[51] while Simon used to make reports calculated to awaken public opinion and written in a style comparable with the minor works of High Victorian Literature. Simon would thus rank as the first of the medical officers to use his position deliberately to influence public opinion towards sanitary improvement. Despite the far greater significance of Simon's position in London, it is clear that this propagandist role of the medical officers was already fully grasped and utilised by the pioneers of Leicester. Both men, as it happened, were as adept in the wielding of the pen as they were with the scalpel and forceps. Barclay wrote copiously on all manner of subjects, and each of them gave lengthy addresses to the town's Literary and Philosophical Society.

Their first report to the Council in February 1847 followed much the same lines as that of George Bown. They stressed the fundamental importance of laying down a proper drainage system. Tampering with the evils of overflowing cesspools or deficient privies and pools of stagnant water in the streets did no lasting good in the absence of effective drainage; 'any system of drainage', they wrote, 'to be beneficial, must be extensive and thoroughly carried out. Your Medical Officers are strongly of the opinion that any system of drainage that is not so will only aggravagate the evil'.[52]

They found the water supply to be generally good except where it, too, reflected the inadequacy of drainage and sewerage in the pollution of wells by neighbouring cesspools. Their strongest censure was, however, reserved for what we would regard as a relatively minor nuisance–that of swine-keeping. In this the Medical Officers reflect their orthodox objection to anything that might pollute the atmosphere. Pythogenic purism demanded the removal of pigs from the vicinity of human habitations. 'The pigsties invariably give rise to most intolerable stenches', they said, 'and those who keep them are tempted to accumulate in great quantity their manure and all sorts of refuse from the streets and elsewhere for sale; thus forming as we judge the foci of disease on a very extensive scale'.[53]

Partly in consequence of this practice of keeping swine in or near dwellings, a multitude of slaughterhouses was to be found in the borough. Buck and Barclay found these 'very objectionable . . . as in many instances the blood and offal was to be swilled down some distance on the open street before a covered drain is reached; and frequently this cleaning is totally neglected, or very inefficiently performed'.[54]

Finally, after adverting to other matters such as inadequately paved streets, they suggested a number of bye-laws to remedy the evils they identified. Before putting these forward, however, they returned to the question of sewerage: 'we would express our decided opinion of the prime necessity of a complete system of drainage, flushing and trapping, for this town, without which it is in vain to expect to raise its mean duration of life to that of the United Kingdom. Earnestly hoping that a Town Drainage Bill may speedily be brought forward and passed into law, our remarks must necessarily be confined to the town in its present state'.[55]

They then proposed five new bye-laws; to prohibit pig-keeping within 30 or 40 feet of any human dwelling; to prohibit the collection of night soil within yards in the borough; to enforce periodic emptying of cesspools and privy holes; to require formation of proper drains in new streets and attention to defective drainage in existing ones, and to ensure that such drains had properly-fitted stench traps.[56]

The fact that modern historians have ignored the appointment of Buck and Barclay in the history of public health is perhaps due to a misleading entry in the table compiled by Dr. Alexander Stewart in his book of 1884.[57] In this he printed the statements of 21 medical officers concerning their own status and remuneration, including their replies to a question on the date of the appointment of the first medical officer in their locality. John Moore, who answered this question in Leicester, gave the date 1849 as the time when John Buck was appointed under the Public Health Act of 1848, evidently regarding the question as applying only to such officers as were approved by the central government.

The appointment of Leicester's medical officers came about because the central government had stipulated the need for professional certification of health risks by qualified medical men. The appointment of Dr. Barclay and Mr. Buck is thus an indication of the growing status of the medical profession. It is also important as marking a trend toward professionalism in local government. Most matters requiring an informed judgement were dealt with by senior members of the Corporation, often with the aid of the Town Clerk, but the Nuisance Removal Acts made this no longer sufficient. The day of the professional expert was at hand. However limited and erroneous their scientific knowledge, the medical officers were regarded by contemporaries as fit and proper persons to advise on the degree of danger posed by all manner of environmental health risks. The signature of qualified medical practitioners would suffice to stop production at a factory, condemn dwelling houses as unfit for human habitation, or require the closure of a slaughter house. To leave elected councillors to make such decisions would invite interminable argument between interested parties where one man's word would be as good as another's; while the trained doctor or surgeon could cloak his decision in the authority of professional expertise.

With the establishment of the Local Board of Health in August 1849 the old Sanitary Committee, which had been appointed on the renewal of the Nuisance Removal Act in 1848, was reconstituted and a new Highways and Sewerage

Committee was created to deal with the more important duties of the Local Board. The work of the two bodies overlapped, however, and the Sanitary Committee was not reappointed in November 1849. The Highways and Sewerage Committee thus became effectively the sole agent of measures concerning improvement and public health in the town, and it was soon recognised as the most important of the various committees of the Council.[58]

Chapter Three

SEWERS AND CENTRALISATION

THE DECISION by the Leicester Corporation to accept a degree of central control under the Public Health Act was not taken lightly. It was one thing to take action against public nuisances and limit the freedom of citizens under local edicts, but it was quite another to submit to the enforcement of such measures at the order of a centralised body, not responsible to the ratepayers.

The notion of bureaucratic interference from Whitehall was generally viewed with horror by local opinion in the provinces. Such hostility was often an instinctive irrational resentment at any interference whatever and sometimes it was grounded in parsimony and a belief that the ratepayers would know best how to spend their own money. Edwin Chadwick, on the other hand, stoutly defended centralisation, as he once told Lyon Playfair: 'Sir, the Devil was expelled from heaven because he objected to centralisation, and all those who object to centralisation oppose it on devilish grounds!'.[1] The record of his dealings with the Council of Leicester leaves little doubt that a prime cause of opposition to Chadwick's centralising proclivities was his own abrasive and insensitive handling of the local authorities.

Initial reaction among Leicester radicals to the notion of central control in the interests of public health was, however, by no means entirely hostile. The issue had raised its head earlier in relation to the establishment of the new Poor Law authority in December 1836. When the first Board of Guardians attempted to operate the Act, it soon came into conflict with the authority of the Poor Law Commission in London. The specific matter of dispute concerned rate collectors, the appointment of whom the Commissioners refused to sanction. In consequence the local Board of Guardians refused to build their new workhouse 'until the guardians understand more definitely what their powers are and what is the will and intention of the Commissioners'.[2] In August the following year the Guardians were again willing to proceed, and in November 1838 the new workhouse was in operation, but the Guardians saw fit in 1839 to petition against the appointment of further Assistant Commissioners because of their lack of local knowledge.[3]

Friction between the local Guardians and Chadwick, the secretary to the Commissioners in London, might well have pre-disposed the Council to look more favourably on the intervention of a central government authority, for the Leicester Guardians were, during their first 10 years of existence, decidedly antipathetic to the liberal views of the Council and in 1840 they even attempted to appoint Thomas Burbidge as clerk to the Leicester Union. When the Poor Law Commissioners refused to sanction his appointment, the Guardians secured, instead, that of his son Joseph.[4]

Three years later allegations of corruption led to an enquiry into the Board's accounts and to the subsequent dismissal of both the relieving officers, one of whom was sentenced to three months imprisonment for his misdemeanours. The Poor Law Commissioners also secured the removal of the workhouse master, and of Joseph Burbidge, and of the auditor whose incompetence had allowed irregularities to pass unchecked.[5]

The contrast in political complexion of the Guardians and the Corporation was largely the result of the peculiar system of voting exercised in elections of the Poor Law Union, which allowed up to 12 votes to the owner-occupiers according to the value of their property. The advantage derived by the Conservatives from this system was not sufficient to deter them from using fraudulent means to secure votes, so that when an enquiry was held into the election of 1845, over 500 Conservative votes were disqualified.[6] As with the unreformed Corporation, the sins of the Conservative administration engendered such public censure that Liberal majorities were assured from that time onwards. The case for central oversight of local affairs had thus been amply vindicated in Leicester, and when Lord Morpeth introduced his Health of Towns Bill in 1847, there was therefore a tacit acceptance in Leicester of the principle of centralised control in matters of public health.

Samuel Stone was careful to point out the implications of Morpeth's Bill: 'Whether the clauses', he wrote, 'giving the Commissioners of Health a veto on the appointment of local surveyors and a power of removal at their pleasure, and depriving the Council of the power to remove any officer with whom they may be dissatisfied, or whether the appointment of Medical Officers by the Commissioners of Health instead of the Council who pay them, are right in principle or may not prove objectionable and vexations in practice are points on which it does not fall within my province to express any opinion'.[7]

Morpeth revised his Bill in response to criticism from the localities and Stone regarded it in March 1848 as 'a much better digested and more carefully prepared' measure. But it still raised the spectre of centralisation, and local councils were ever jealous of their independence. Stone likened the proposed Central Board to the Commissioners of the Poor Law, but he recognised that efficient working of the Act probably required a competent central authority 'with somewhat extensive powers!'.[8] A Council committee appointed to consider the Bill drew attention to the same issue: 'The problem to be solved—the difficulty to be overcome—is to reconcile the existence of a Central Board with the independence of local government'.[9]

The committee pointed out that the Bill as it then stood required the approval of the General Board in London 'to every appointment or removal of local officers, except the Clerk or treasurer in incorporated boroughs—to the construction or discontinuance of every sewer—to every contract to the extent of £200—and to the exercise of almost every power vested in the local Board of Health'.[10] The position of the localities was therefore to be closely patterned on the relationship of the Guardians of the Poor to the Poor Law Commissions. The Council committee therefore expressed the view that several provisions of the Act should be modified and that apart from acting as an arbiter in disputes between the local boards and other interests, the powers of the General Board should be limited 'to the approval of money to be borrowed and to the general scheme of sewerage proposed'.[11] It was precisely this power to approve borrowing which Chadwick regarded as the lynch-pin of his authority at the General Board, and which was to give rise to considerable frustrations in Leicester and to protracted friction with the authorities in London.

Whetstone persuaded the Council not to oppose the Bill, but simply to call for its modification. When in due course the cholera epidemic of 1848 and the propaganda of Edwin Chadwick and the Health of Towns Association led to the passing of the Public Health Act, the Council sought its application to Leicester. It is possible that one reason for this was the fear that the Act might be imposed upon the town because of its high rate of mortality, since this exceeded the proportion of 23 per 1,000 and the General Board was therefore empowered to carry out an official enquiry if it saw fit. To Whetstone and the sanitary reformers of Leicester who had campaigned for so long for a comprehensive sewerage plan, the Act offered the prospect of realising their aims without any costly private legislation.

As a preliminary move toward applying the Act to Leicester, the General Board sent one of its inspectors, William Ranger, to view and make a report on the town. The diagnosis and the remedy were equally predictable. High mortality resulting from accumulations of filth could only be cured by adequate drainage. Ranger even quantified the excess deaths attributable to the sanitary defects of the town. In the three years 1840 to 1842 he calculated that 1,489 deaths had resulted above the 3,056 which would have occurred if the town's death rate of three per cent. had been no more than the two per cent. which obtained in healthier parts of the country.[12]

First among the causes of Leicester's high mortality was 'a want of sub-drainage'. The meadows surrounding the town to the north, east and west were never dry, while an extensive withy bed close to the castle was generally under water. The architect, William Flint, described to Ranger the 'basins' formed by embankments surrounding courtyards of houses, where rainwater mixed with liquid refuse to generate 'noxious effluvia'. In Greatholme Street to the west of the town 'the basins dip towards the houses, and the water is consequently conducted into and under the walls, whence they are always saturated'. Elsewhere the 'offensive matter from privy holes passes into the unoccupied grounds, and stands in pools upon the surface'.[13] There could be no doubt of the prime need for a complete new system of drainage: Ranger was evidently delighted to find this truth already accepted by public opinion in the town. The medical officers, in particular, had 'shown themselves to be thorough sanitary advocates. Nothing can surpass the attention and zeal displayed by these gentlemen', said Ranger, and he concluded that 'this place forms one in which the measures of the Public Health Act cannot fail to produce an extraordinary change for the better'.[14]

In June, Ranger's report was sent to the Council containing proposals for complete and efficient sanitary works. A committee was set up to study this, but it is evident from the tone of its recommendations that there was a certain resentment owing to Ranger's unsolicited advice on how to set about the drainage and sewerage of the town. The committee noted that the Council was not 'bound by any of the recommendations contained in the report of Mr. Ranger',[15] but it saw no reason to oppose the confirmatory Act of Parliament. It went on to record its opinion, 'that it will be expedient to employ some competent Civil Engineer in order that he may lay down some practical scheme for the guidance of the Council in carrying this act into operation'.[16] The engineer chosen was Thomas Wicksteed, and his appointment was confirmed on 5 September 1849.

The choice was in some respects singularly unfortunate and boded ill for future relations with the General Board, for Wicksteed had publicly taken issue with Chadwick over the operation of water supplies.[17] The Council at Leicester was apparently not aware of this and chose him purely on the strength of his professional reputation. Under the terms of the Public Health Act, the Council itself constituted the Local Board of Health, and the first communication from Whitehall to the Local Board in Leicester was a mild rebuke on the grounds that the appointment of John Buck as Medical Officer on 8 August was 'premature', as the Board has not yet prescribed the duties of such an Officer of Health.[18] Centralisation was already coming into conflict with the independence of a vigorous local authority.

The establishment of the Local Board of Health and the Highways and Sewerage Committee marks the greatest single development in the expansion of local government in 19th-century Leicester, if we except the establishment of the School Board which was not absorbed by the Corporation till 1902. The standing committees on Finance, Estates and Markets had carried on much the same routine work as under the old Corporation, though with more energy, frugality and attention to detail. The Watch Committee, established in 1836 to shape and control the police force, continued its work also, but its duties were increasingly routine with sporadic flurries of excitement as the Chartists had their day and new head constables were appointed. The principal growth point of local government was in relation to problems of urban concentration: overcrowding, lack of adequate water supply and sanitation, and industrial pollution. These were the problems which fell to the lot of the Local Board of Health and its Highways and Sewerage Committee.

Sewage disposal was the kernel of the problem of public health or sanitary reform, as it was called. Joseph Whetstone, who remained chairman of the Highways and Sewerage Committee from its inception till his death in 1868, insisted throughout the debate over improvement on the primacy of sewerage in the Council's list of priorities. Dr. Barclay and Mr. Buck reinforced the message in their reports, whilst the town's high mortality was seen as the direct result of delay in attending to the deficiencies of the existing sewerage.

On a national level Chadwick's Report of 1842 had pressed home the same theme that good water supply and sewerage were prerequisites of public health. In 1840, even before the publication of the report, the Registrar General had emphasised the close relationship between drainage and disease. 'If a survey were made', he wrote, 'of the districts of the metropolis, and the levels, the sewers, the drains, and the nuisances known to be pernicious were accurately laid down upon a map it would agree very remarkably with the table of relative mortality'.[19]

Chadwick had very decided notions on sewerage as on most things. He summarised his ideas in 1854, as putting in place of 'brick sewers in every street large enough for men to go up, a system of sewers graduated in size, each line being proportionate to the quantity of drainage provided for; so arranged as to concentrate and hasten the flow, instead of diffusing it over a wide surface, and thereby retarding it; impermeable and therefore preventing the escape of sewer fluid; self-cleansing, instead of accumulating deposits, and consequently avoiding for the most part the necessity of flushing; a system which, as contrasted with the former, may be described as one of continuous flow instead of stagnation'.[20] Wicksteed shared this belief in glazed pipes, writing in his report that 'for all sewers of 12 inches in diameter, and under, if the cost of glazed earthenware be the same as good brickwork in cement, the former would I consider be most suitable; . . . for all drains connected with dwelling houses, they should undoubtedly be used in preference, and will I have no doubt be found cheaper than any other'.[21]

Yet when in September 1850 Wicksteed presented his plans for a complete system of sewerage and drainage, the General Board of Health met them with obstruction and hostility. On the morning that the Leicester Sewerage Bill came before the House of Commons Committee, Chadwick sent a long letter objecting that it gave borrowing powers without the prior consent of the General Board.[22] The Bill, duly altered, received Royal Assent, and on 20 August application was made to the General Board for permission to borrow £35,000 to undertake the works. Thereafter delay followed delay. Despite Wicksteed's offer to amplify and clarify his plans, and despite urgent appeals from the town clerk for a speedy decision, nothing was heard from the General Board till November, when Chadwick sent one of his own inspectors, William Lee, to make his own report on the sewerage of Leicester.[23]

The Sewerage Scheme Rejected

When Lee's report was finally presented in February 1852, it proved to be an unqualified condemnation of Wicksteed's scheme.[24] Lee criticised Wicksteed's calculation of the amount of rain water likely to flow through the sewers, saying it would 'require seventeen hours to discharge two-thirds of an inch of rain' so that water would be penned up and 'the sewers gorged from the engine sewer, all up the mains and under the town'.[25] In the event this criticism proved remarkably accurate, but at the time it was obscured by the more trivial and tendentious arguments over the size of Wicksteed's pipes, which Lee thought too large for the subsidiary sewers, and over his use of a double course of bricks in the main channel, which Lee regarded as unnecessary. Lee also doubted the efficacy of the proposed purification plant. At the same time Lee favoured a twin network of sewers so that some could utilise the natural fall of the land, while only the low-lying areas would need to be artificially drained. His report thus appeared to consist of trifling criticisms and misplaced parsimony, for, as Wicksteed pointed out, the construction of two separate systems would in fact cost a great deal more than one comprehensive network.

To the Local Board such treatment at the hands of the General Board must have seemed utterly perverse. Repeated delays and want of courtesy and then the rejection of costly plans drawn up by a prominent engineer must have confirmed all the Council's fears of centralised bureaucracy.

It was widely believed that the opposition of the General Board arose out of spite because its own inspectorate had not been asked to draw up the plans. However, a solution presented itself in the form of arbitration and both reports were accordingly submitted to Robert Stephenson, the railway engineer.

Stephenson's report was presented in May 1852 substantially vindicating Wicksteed's proposals against the criticisms raised by Lee. Stephenson diplomatically rapped both the Leicester Board and the General Board over the knuckles for what he called 'the thread of acrimony running through the negotiations',[26] but his remarks were aimed primarily at the attitude of the General Board. This, he said, was 'altogether undignified and unworthy' of a body 'especially appointed to encourage and forward, and not to thwart and delay, or as it has sometimes happened within my knowledge, altogether to stop improvements of a sanitary character, because they do not come quite up to their empirical standard, or are not carried out according to their particular system, which it is notorious does not in all cases meet with the approval of practical men'.[27]

Even after this judgement by Robert Stephenson, the Board continued to ask for further details on the construction of subsidiary sewers and the position of the sewage works. Not until October 1852 did the Board finally sanction the borrowing of funds for the main sewerage. It is scarcely surprising that this delay created deep frustration and resentment in Leicester. 'It is trifling with the common weal of a large community thus to prolong discussions and enquiry, which everybody except the Superintending Inspectors of the General Board thinks have been carried on to the utmost limits of endurance; and that at a season when the mortality of the town is unprecedented and the approach of a dire plague is anticipated',[28] wrote James Thompson, editor of the *Leicester Chronicle*. To Thompson, the prevarication and procrastinations of the General Board were personified in the apostle of centralisation, Edwin Chadwick. When, five years later, it was announced that he was to receive an annual pension of £1,000 on his retirement, the paper asked if he had not already received a liberal salary for his labours. His case, it said, was 'a singularly unhappy one for the exemplification of the principle of granting pensions'. Why, asked Thompson, should other public servants, such as 'worn out editors' be expected to do without, while 'your well-feathered functionary of the Order of Red Tape must be extravagantly paid for doing nothing to the end of his days'.[29]

Despite the tendentious nature of much of Lee's report he did single out one crucial fault in Wicksteed's plans; namely the tendency for water to back up the storm water overflow channel in time of heavy rain, exposing cellars in the lower parts of the town to periodic inundation with polluted water. As time went on, this fault became increasingly serious, and it is difficult to understand how Robert Stephenson could have overlooked this aspect of Lee's criticism.

The Water Supply

Edwin Chadwick's opposition to Wicksteed originated in their dispute over the technique of water supply. In common with many engineers at the time, Wicksteed doubted the feasibility of bringing water long distances to be used at constant pressure over a wide area. Outlets close to the supply would, he thought, receive water at the expense of those further removed. Wicksteed told the commissioners enquiring into the state of large towns in 1845 that 'when water is forced through pipes, either by a natural or artificial head . . . friction is created in proportion to the velocity of the water and by the length of the line of pipes. As the distances increase the power must either be increased or the velocity reduced: . . . those houses which were near the source would have abundant supply while those at a distance would have a very small supply if any'.[30]

At this time Chadwick was an admirer of Thomas Hawkesley, who had provided Nottingham with an excellent supply of water from the Trent since 1829. Hawkesley became engineer to the Leicester Waterworks Company, and continued to advise on the town's water supply till his death in 1892. Wicksteed took issue with Hawkesley not only over the practicability of constant as opposed to intermittent supply of water, but also over Hawkesley's plan to bring water to the town from Thornton, a village nine miles north-west of Leicester. At the time, this was a most ambitious proposal. When Hawkesley first suggested it in 1846, no town had gone so far for supplies or collected them in so great a reservoir. Many doubted if his plans were practicable. In 1847, however, Manchester Corporation decided to construct a reservoir at Longdendale, 20 miles east in the Pennines; it came into use in 1851 and was the first of many such schemes adopted by large towns in the second half of the 19th century.[31]

The novelty of the Thornton project was sufficient to deter many prospective investors and Chadwick's original company collapsed. Whetstone had always favoured a municipal initiative in the matter, but the Public Health Act clearly stated that it was illegal for a Local Board 'to construct or lay down any waterworks within such limits, if and so long as any such Company shall be able and willing to lay on Water . . . upon such terms as shall be certified to be reasonable by the General Board of Health'.[32]

To resolve this deadlock a compromise was agreed upon whereby the Corporation undertook to guarantee a four per cent. dividend to the Waterworks Company for the first 30 years of its existence. In return for this, the Corporation was to receive a share of any profit above £4 10s. 0d. per cent, in addition to the interest on the 680 £25 shares which the Corporation agreed to purchase in the Company.

These provisions caused consternation at the General Board, William Ranger damning the Bill as 'opposed both to the letter and spirit of the Public Health Act'.[33] It is difficult to sympathise with this view. The Act excluded direct involvement by the Local Board *so long as* a private company was able and willing to supply the water, and this was not the case. Local opposition was voiced, particularly against the 'guarantee clause' and on the grounds that the proposed supply would be insufficient, 'in proof of which it is only necessary to state', wrote John Windley, 'that some of the parties now holding shares are actually giving them away to free themselves of the odium and responsibility attaching to them'.[34] There is no evidence to substantiate this assertion by Windley, but it is certainly in accord with the dispirited accounts of the shareholders' meeting given in the local press, prior to the agreement with the Corporation.

With the financial backing of the Corporation, however, the project proceeded, and the Leicester Waterworks Amendment Act was passed in 1851, incorporating and altering where necessary the Act of 1847. The Corporation as Local Board of Health exercised the right to appoint to the Company's board four directors, of whom Joseph Whetstone was one.

After a few years the town began to receive a steady income from its investment in what proved to be a highly successful company, which furnished a plentiful supply of pure water for the needs of the town, though, inevitably, further supplies had to be found as the population multiplied.

Re-cycling the Sewage

While there was fundamental disagreement between Chadwick and Wicksteed over the mode of operating water supplies, they both shared an enthusiasm for the potential value of town sewage. Indeed, it is ironic that the General Board found itself so much at odds with the man who above all others endeavoured to turn Chadwick's dream of profitable sewage into reality. Where town refuse was concerned, they shared a belief in the old adage: 'Where there's muck, there's money'.

One object of Chadwick's Towns Improvement Company was to supply sewage in a liquid form as manure to local farmers and in 1849 he wrote a treatise on 'Sewer Manure' for the Metropolitan Sewers Commission.[35] Wicksteed's interest in the matter apparently dates from 1845 when he was called upon to report on the possibility of making profitable use of the sewage of London. He brought forward a scheme, at the suggestion of Professor Aikin of Guy's

Hospital, for the separation of solid matter by lime. In 1851, he took out a patent for the manufacture of sewage manure which earned the approval of Robert Stephenson and others. After experiments which proved 'highly successful', he formed the Patent Solid Sewage Manufacturing Company in order to conduct works on a large scale at Leicester.

Thus when Wicksteed agreed to construct a sewerage network for the Corporation it was with a view to providing the raw material for his own private investment in the Sewage Company. There were in the sewerage scheme three main sewers constructed of circular sections and varying between 56 and 15 inches in diameter. One of these ran from west of the river Soar in Braunstone Gate northwards to the district known as Woodgate and thence across the river to St. Margaret's Pasture, where a short section of main sewer met the needs of the densely-populated area of Northgates and Frog Island. The second main sewer commenced below the Royal Infirmary to the south of the town, followed the course of Asylum Street to the site of the present Polytechnic building in the Newarke, wound its way through the old castle grounds and then ran close to the river along Bath Lane before swinging eastward towards Allsaints Church and down Sanvey Gate to Watling Street, where it was joined by the third main artery from Uppingham Road. This last was the most tortuous of the three main routes, incorporating four right-angled bends before it reached Russell Square on Wharf Street, where it swung north-west to Belgrave Gate and then down Burley's Lane to Watling Street. From their junction in Watling Street, the eastern and central main sewers turned due north to link with that from the west. United into one, the channel then cut straight across Abbey meadow to a point just to the west of the river Soar. From here, the sewage was taken under it in a cast-iron pipe and then raised 24 feet by steam pumps to settling tanks.

In April 1853, the Company's formal contract to lift and disinfect the sewage was accepted, and it began operations two years later. The works were noteworthy in several respects. It was the first known instance where an artificial

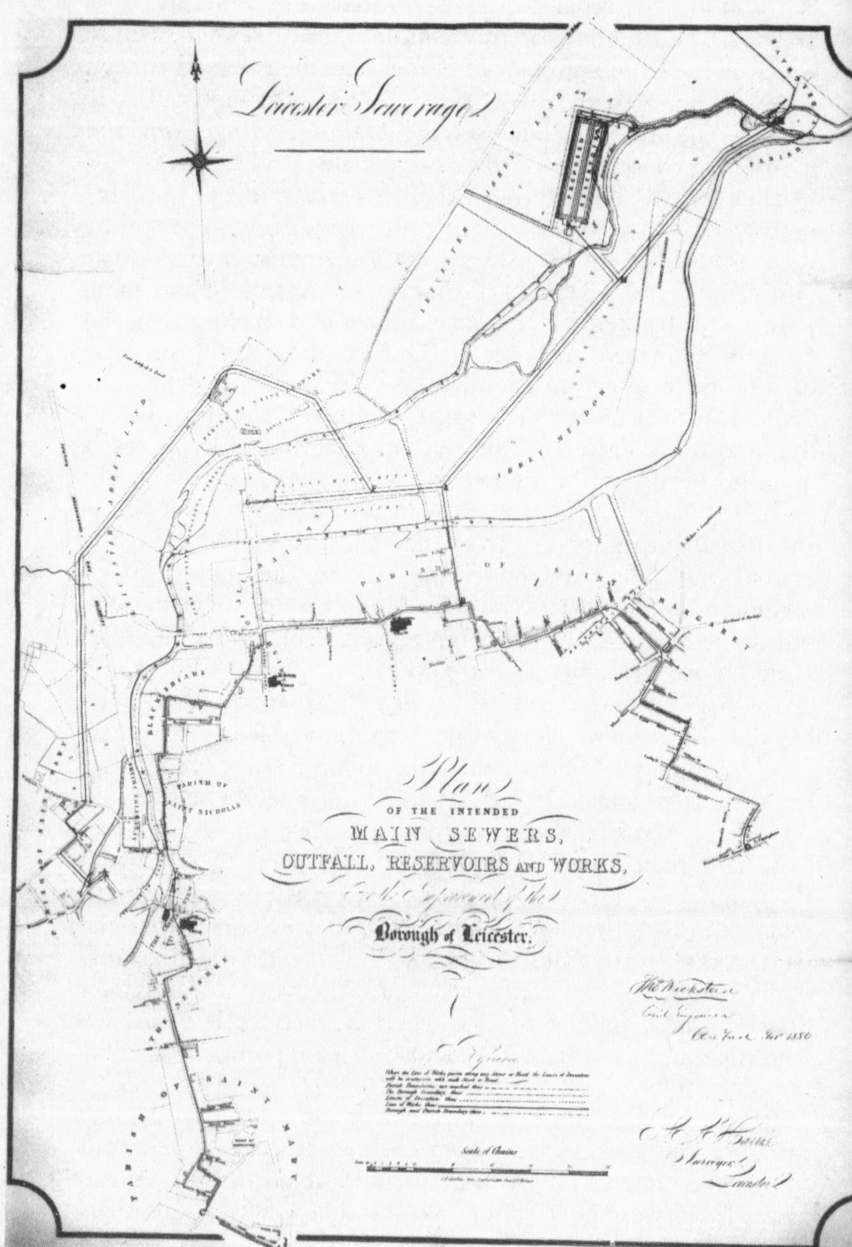

Fig. 3. Sewerage map of 1850

outfall was obtained for the sewage of an entire town, though there had been some attempt to lift sewage by steam pumps on a smaller scale at Edinburgh.[36] More important to Wicksteed was Professor Aikin's method of processing the raw sewage. The method was to inject lime into the slurry as it entered the tanks, causing precipitation of the solid matter. This was raised from the floor of the settling tanks by an archimedian screw to drying areas above, while the clear effluent was returned to the river free from any odour—according to Wicksteed, 'not only in an inoffensive state but in a drinkable state'.[37]

The *Leicester Chronicle* jubilantly proclaimed that 'Mr. Inspector Lee' despite his fears as to the efficacy of the deodorising plant, 'might have washed his hands in the water at the outlet for the purified sewage, without requiring a supplementary rinse in eau de cologne'.[38]

The works appeared to be highly successful. Wicksteed informed parliament in 1853, 'that he had a manufactury (*sic*) at work at Leicester for the last twelve months where the sullage from the filthiest sewers in the town had been purified, the fertilising matter precipitated, and the water discharged into the river free from all noxious matter'.[39]

Chadwick himself visited them and was duly impressed. Deputations came from Coventry and other towns to view the operations. The Company entertained visitors from Europe and even a 'gentleman from Bombay', who came to see the works;[40] while the Corporation was well pleased with an arrangement which relieved it of all expense and even offered the prospect of financial gain in the future. But, alas! the project was an economic failure.

Wicksteed had foreseen prices of £2 a ton as the market value of the manure, based upon the current high prices charged for Peruvian Guano, which he maintained it equalled or excelled. He soon encountered considerable sales resistance, however, manifested in ever-growing stocks of unsold manure. The price fell to below its cost price, but market demand proved singularly inelastic. Wicksteed maintained a bold front, inviting the Council to issue a public statement expressing its satisfaction with his works. But at the same time he was quick to cover himself under the Limited Liability Act of 1855. By the summer of 1858 funds were exhausted and the Company gave notice of its intention to relinquish the works to the Council.[41]

The Corporation thus became the owners of an undertaking which lost them an average of £2,000 per year. (According to John Buck, the works involved a capital outlay of £30,000.) The price of its manure fell to a shilling a ton, and at one stage the Council were obliged to give it away in order to dispose of unsold stocks—an action which made it doubly difficult to obtain a reasonable price thereafter.[42] As for Wicksteed and his partners, they had 'lost all faith in the practicability of converting sewage into valuable manure', as one of them wrote to Samuel Stone.[43]

Nevertheless, attempts continued to be made. A Mr. Kirkman pestered the Council for permission to apply his own process for the treatment of town waste for a number of years. His optimism was not matched by practical ability however, and his efforts ended in the ignominy of proceedings for bankruptcy.[44]

In the event, William Lee's criticism of the plan devised by Wicksteed was justified so far as the discharge of storm water was concerned. Wicksteed had constructed an overflow channel at the artificial outfall before the sewage was conducted under the river. As Lee predicted, however, in time of flood, the river water flowed up this overflow channel from its outlet below Belgrave Mill, forcing the contents of the sewers in the town back up into the cellars and ground floor rooms of houses in the low-lying districts.

Pail Closets Introduced

There is no doubt that within the space of 30 years the network laid down by Wicksteed was seriously overloaded. In that time the 60,000 inhabitants of 1851 had doubled to over 120,000, while the Board of Health demanded that every new building be connected where possible to the main sewerage network. Pressure was alleviated in 1872 by the introduction of the 'Rochdale system' for the removal of night soil. This meant the use of pail closets instead of the further extension of water closets.

What appears to be a retrograde step was taken on the advice of Dr. Clarke, a member of the Highways and Sewerage Committee, with the full approval of Dr. Wyatt Crane, the Medical Officer of Health, and the Borough Surveyor. Clarke wanted to reduce the evil of overflowing cesspools that still abounded in the more densely populated parts of the town. He suggested that a more effective means of dealing with the problem was called for than gradually substituting water closets. These, he pointed out, were liable to be out of order through the action of frost for several weeks each winter; and as they were flushed by water carried in buckets for some distance the work of cleansing them was often imperfectly performed. Clarke concluded, 'it is apparent that the water closet system mainly breaks down with the wretchedly poor and improvident, and with those who will take no care'.[45]

The sub-committee set up to enquire into the matter examined the pail or tub closets used in Halifax, Rochdale, Manchester, Salford and Nottingham. It recommended a trial of the Manchester and Rochdale system in some of the crowded courts on Sanvey Gate and Palmerston Street. The result of these experiments led to the rejection of the Manchester system as 'more costly and objectionable to sitters on privy seats',[46] and likely to perpetuate undue accumulation in ashpits which could pollute the water of nearby wells. The Rochdale system, which utilised galvanised buckets containing some disinfectant, apparently excluded 'most if not all these difficulties and by ensuring a systematic removal without application from the people, is in a sanitary point of view, the best system', said the committee, 'for promoting the purity of the air surrounding the houses in the courts and poorer districts'.[47] However, it had been apparent for some years that a more radical solution would eventually become necessary. Pail closets were never more than a short-term expedient.

Sewage Irrigation and the Beaumont Leys Farm

By 1869 the argument concerning the treatment of the town's sewage had resolved itself into one over the merits and demerits of irrigation. The Council invited Mr. Baldwin Latham, an eminent engineer, to report on the possibility of utilising sewage in this way, and in April 1870 Latham presented his 'carefully written and well-reasoned report on the whole subject'.[48] James Thompson gave him unwavering support in the pages of the *Leicester Chronicle*, devoting editorials to this subject almost to the exclusion of every other topic.

The Council on the other hand had a natural desire to utilise its existing works if at all possible, and in 1871 it granted a 21-year lease of the works to the Phosphate Sewage Company which aimed to purify the sewage by a chemical process different from that used by Wicksteed.[49] Thompson regarded this hope as a delusion, and condemned the agreement as a 'precipitate, ill considered, and unwise proceeding'.[50] The *Leicester Journal* on the other hand saw great advantages in the proposal 'which secures very considerable advantages to the ratepayers, by saving them from an indefinite and ruinous outlay of capital for an ever-expanding system of farming by sewage irrigation'. The latter it regarded as 'crude and unprofitable'. It attacked the editor of the *Chronicle* as 'that self-deluded irrigationist ex-councillor James Thompson', and warned its readers that 'if once these mountebank riders of an irrigation hobby are permitted to start, they will continue to run their races at the public expense'.[51]

The *Journal's* uncritical acceptance of the claims of the Phosphate Sewage Company was ill-founded. The *Chronicle* gave warning that the arrangement would ultimately prove unsatisfactory, and that litigation would follow. 'The Corporation', it said, 'will assuredly have to retrace its steps before a very long period has elapsed. The bargain is a mere makeshift—a temporary expedient to escape from a dilemma. Much better would it have been at once to introduce the Irrigation Scheme, for to that conclusion must the Corporation come at last'.[52]

So indeed it did. Negotiations with the Phosphate Company broke off in September 1873, when its terms were seen to be totally unacceptable. It was generally acknowledged by this time that Wicksteed's system was seriously deficient in the capacity of the main outlet and that there was a pressing need to lower the course of the river to the north of the town in order to drain the low-lying districts effectively. In view of this the Highways and Sewerage Committee offered a prize of 200 guineas for the best scheme for dealing with the sewerage and storm waters of the town. The Council decided in favour of a plan by J. B. Everard and sought parliamentary authority to carry out a modified version of his plan.[53] Everard's scheme was, however, strongly attacked by the Government Inspector, Major Tulloch, since it would continue to involve considerable expense in pumping the sewage and the filtration beds would be too close to the growing district of Belgrave.[54] In June 1875, Sir Joseph Bazalgette, the most eminent sanitary engineer of his time, advanced a scheme for joint action with the adjacent sanitary authorities, but they were unable to share the initial costs of the scheme, and Bazalgette thereupon made his proposals to the borough alone, recommending the purchase of 800 acres for irrigation between Barkby Wharf and Sileby Mill. Bazalgette put the cost of his plan at about £300,000–an expense that the Council hesitated to incur, and the question was again postponed.[55] Meanwhile, the relief accorded to the sewage system by pail closets was extended by the addition of four new settling tanks on 10 acres of land adjacent to the old sewage works in 1877.[56]

Complaints about the state of the river below Leicester were again serious in the summer of 1884, and the Local Government Board sent Major Tulloch to conduct an inquiry into the matter. The Corporation defended its record and proved that a remarkably good effluent was produced by the sewage works, but the state of the river below Belgrave was admittedly deplorable and the Local Government Board urged immediate action to remedy this.[57]

Joseph Gordon, The Borough Surveyor from Stephen's death in 1881, had in fact already prepared a comprehensive report containing eight alternative schemes for tackling the problem.[58] Whilst this was being discussed news came of an offer by the owner of the Beaumont Leys Estate to sell or lease his land to the Corporation for sewage irrigation. Beaumont Leys lay to the north-west of the town on an area of high ground from which good drainage could be obtained into the valley of the Rothley Brook. After some further consultation with Major Tulloch it was decided to proceed with the Beaumont Leys scheme, though in the meantime the owner had died and his heir proved much less accommodating. By August 1885 the acquisition of Beaumont Leys received approval of the Local Government Board and Gordon proceeded at once to lay out the land for sewage irrigation, the biggest scheme of its kind in the country.[59]

In order to convey the contents of the sewers to the farm a new pumping station was erected at the old sewage works. Messrs. Gimson and Company supplied the four huge beam engines and pumps which raised the sewage 164ft. through twin 33-inch rising mains to 1,334 acres of farm land over which it was distributed by a network of irrigation channels. Stockdale Harrison, a local architect whose firm later designed the De Montfort Hall, was responsible for designing the pumping station itself.

Had it not been for Gordon's relaying of the trunk sewers there would probably still have been complaints from the residents of Belgrave and Thurmaston. As it was, however, the new works proved a complete success and the efficiency of the sewage farm was soon 'taken for granted',[60] while its fields provided food for local hospitals and other satisfied customers until the opening of the present Wanlip Works in 1963. There is little doubt that in Joseph Gordon Leicester had a brilliant engineer as its Borough Surveyor. Unlike his predecessor, he wisely refused to be at the beck and call of every committee chairman, and conserved his energies for major works in his charge. He retired in July 1889 and took up the post of Chief Engineer of the London County Council, 'the blue riband' of his profession as it was described at the time; but he unfortunately collapsed and died a fortnight later.[61]

The success of sewage irrigation has met with some criticism in recent years on account of the supposed pollution of the soil. Indeed when, in 1965, Leicester Corporation closed their sewage farm and opened a new works at Wanlip for the processing of the town's waste, its plans to build a housing estate on the irrigated lands came to a halt because of fears over toxic levels of metal pollution in the soil.

In fact analysis proved that the problem was not connected with irrigation by sewage as such, but was caused by domestic waste water containing zinc oxide from baby powders and by the washing into the drains of lead deposits from car exhausts. It was these metallic elements and not the human effluent which raised fears of soil pollution at Beaumont Leys.[62]

Chapter Four

THE LOCAL BOARD OF HEALTH

WHILE THE WATER SUPPLY and sewage works provided two of the town's vital amenities, the Local Board concerned itself with a wide range of other matters through its Medical Officer and Inspector of Nuisances. John Buck resigned as Medical Officer in 1853 to take up an appointment as Medical Superintendent of the County Lunatic Asylum, housed in what is now the central block of the University. He was replaced by John Moore, a surgeon who was an alderman at the time, a fact which occasioned some adverse criticism. Moore left the Council and must have devoted the greater part of his time to his duties as Medical Officer for the rest of his life. In fact it seems clear that he underestimated the burden of the office and worked himself into an early grave.[1] He never asked for a rise in his salary of £100 per year, partly because of the feeling of insecurity which accompanies old age in jobs without a pension, and partly because he was one of the generation of reforming radicals who were dedicated to municipal economy.[2] Indeed he himself had voted to reduce the salary of the Borough Surveyor from £150 to £130 when it was fixed in 1849. Meanwhile, George Bown was forced to retire through ill health, and in 1849 Sergeant Joseph Wright took his place as Inspector of Nuisances, being relieved from his normal work for the Constabulary.[3]

Enlightened opinion in the town recognised the achievements of the Board and its medical officers. Joseph Dare wrote in 1849: 'I trace their steps in almost every locality, leaving in their course blessings more substantial than the fabled gifts of the deities of olden times. Pigsties, drains, cesspools, and many other similar nuisances have been removed in all these more obvious situations, and, no doubt, time will reveal those that at present lie out of sight'.[4]

Although Dare continued to toss such bouquets to the Board in his annual reports to the Domestic Mission, the majority of comment from the public was in the form of complaint that something had not been done; for instance that refuse had not been collected, or middens effectively emptied. Such complaints indicate that the Board was increasingly regarded as the proper authority to look after such matters. Its positive achievements were taken for granted.

The activity which led to the most frequent complaint and remonstrance by poorer citizens was the suppression of swine-keeping. Barclay and Buck had singled out the practice of keeping pigs near dwelling houses as the nuisance which called 'most imperatively for immediate remedy'.[5]

The bye-law specified a minimum distance of 30ft. from any dwelling, and wherever the practice of pig-keeping was deemed a danger to health, the medical officer would sign a certificate to that effect and the owners would then be ordered to remove the swine within a limited period, usually 14 days. What degree of hardship this kind of action caused to the poor is very difficult to estimate. One has no means of telling how important the sale of pigs would be to the average family. But it is clear from the number of petitions presented against orders to remove swine that many considered the effects a serious financial loss. John English presented a memorial signed by 21 of his neighbours against an order to remove his pigs within a month. Three other people presented a similar petition from neighbours who stated that they had no objection to and did not experience any annoyance from these pigs. Buck, however, reported that the case was a bad one and 'several of those who have signed the memorial are persons who had complained of the nuisance'.[6]

Buck and Barclay were well aware of the resentment caused by their policy and it probably goes far to explain the 'odium and abuse' which they say they incurred in their labours.[7] They did not regard the keeping of swine as a real source of income to the poor so much as a sort of nest-egg or reserve of capital to rely on in hard times. 'We find', they wrote, 'the poor generally aware that they cannot fatten a pig with any profit, but they appear rather to regard it as a deposit for little sums that are willingly given out of their earnings for this purpose, when trade is good. Our interference has in some instances, appeared a great hardship to the industrious poor, but our duty has obliged us to insist on their removal'.[8]

Linked with the existence of pig-keeping were the great number of slaughterhouses, to which the medical officers frequently referred. The pigs fed on offal from the animals killed and thus formed a useful complement to such places. Moore stated in 1855 that: 'Out of sixty-two slaughter houses I visited I found thirty-nine kept pigs for the purpose of consuming blood offal, the swill tubs in connection with these I consider form one of the greatest nuisances of the slaughterhouses'.[9]

Sanitarian obsession with foul smells sometimes led the medical officers and the Local Board into ludicrous situations. The Rev. Robert Burnaby of St. George's Church complained that his sister had been ill for a whole day entirely on account of the fumes of turpentine used in the making of rubberised fabrics in a nearby factory, and his assertion was supported by the signed testimony of a local doctor, C. R. Crossley, who later sat on the Council as a Tory member.[10] If we can sympathise with Miss Burnaby, it is surely difficult to feel sorry for the employees of a firm in Market Street who complained of the 'sickly effluvia' of roasting coffee. Nevertheless, the Officer of Health solemnly agreed to see if the fumes could not be turned into the chimney.[11]

The medical officers exhibited a similar propensity to tilt at windmills in the so-called 'offensive trades'. Tripe boilers, gut cleaners, and tallow-makers all excited disapproval on account of the foul smells associated with their business operations and were frequently obliged to modify or close their premises. The disapproval of the medical officer was often sufficient to prevent the establishment of such unwelcome trades in the town. Buck noted an instance as early as December 1849:

> Although we were recently threatened with an irruption of Gut dressers or sausage envelope manufacturers, as they styled themselves, from the Surrey side of the Metropolis, I am happy to add that after two or three unsuccessful attempts to locate themselves, we succeeded in banishing them and their business I trust for ever from Leicester.[12]

Dr. John Snow refuted the scientific basis of the pythogenic case in his evidence to a parliamentary enquiry in 1855. Snow argued that many of the so-called offensive trades 'really do not assist in the propagation of epidemic diseases, and that in fact they are not injurious to the public health'. If they had been injurious, he considered that they would have been 'extremely so to the workmen engaged in those trades', which was not in fact the case.[13] As with the suppression of pig-keeping, official disapproval of offensive trades resulted in the reduction of unpleasant smells suffered by the community at large, and as most medical men still held that evil smells betrayed the existence of 'fatal miasma', the removal of such odiferous operators was at any rate a good exercise in public relations for the health authorities.

The Inspection of Industrial Premises

An area in which conflict might have been expected to arise was that of regulating factory and workshop conditions. John Moore, the Medical Officer, reported in 1861 on the remarks of John Simon, the Medical Officer to the Privy Council, concerning an alleged high rate of mortality from pulmonary disease in Leicester.[14] This high incidence of pulmonary disease was the subject of a special report to the Privy Council based on the investigations of Dr. Greenhow. Moore pointed out that the calculations Dr. Greenhow used were based upon an average of the seven-year period from 1848 to 1854, though his official visit to Leicester took place in October 1860. Even on the basis of those figures Leicester was by no means exceptional in its rate of mortality from pulmonary disease. From Greenhow's statistics it could be shown that Leicester was sixteenth in the list of 28 towns or town districts having populations at the census of 1851 of 50,000 or upwards. Thus Moore showed that there was nothing particularly alarming in the death rate of 64 per 1,000 from this class of disease which was calculated for Leicester. (In Liverpool the figure was 100 per 1,000 and the rates for Nottingham, West Derby, Birmingham, Bristol, Leeds, Manchester, Salford, Blackburn, Wolverhampton, Stoke-on-Trent, Newcastle, Preston, Sheffield, and Macclesfield were all greater than that for Leicester.) The point of Dr. Greenhow's report or the message Simon contrived to read into it was that something ought to be done to improve conditions in the workshops of Leicester which contributed to the growth of pulmonary disease. 'It appears', wrote Simon, 'that in Leicester to a great extent, the Manufacturing occupations are followed in an impure atmosphere; that probably half the local manufacture is carried on in the dwellings of the workpeople, or in workshops constructed by the conversion of dwelling-houses; that here commonly the rooms are small and ill-ventilated, as well as sometimes overcrowded; and that even where employment is in factories, the rooms allotted to various large branches of industry are in many instances overcrowded or ill-ventilated, or both overcrowded and ill-ventilated'. Simon recognised that the Local Board could do nothing to diminish the length of the working day, but suggested that 'everything possible under existing laws should be done to prevent the overcrowding of dwellings and workplaces, to provide proper residences for the labouring classes, and to enforce everywhere wholesome ventilation and cleanliness'.

Moore acknowledged the desirability of Simon's objectives, but he questioned Simon's assumption that the Local Board had sufficient authority to procure improvement in the condition of workshops, factories and dwelling houses. 'In the first place', said Moore, 'the Board possess no power to prevent the overcrowding of dwelling-houses, where the occupiers consist of only one family'. They did, however, 'take special care that byelaws regulating the height and size of rooms, and the required spare ground to each house for securing ventilation, are duly complied with'. 'There is no existing law', said Moore, 'to prevent overcrowding of workshops. The improvement of ventilation is nearly all that the Board can accomplish, and this is a subject surrounded with difficulties.'

An example of these difficulties was provided in the premises of a hosier in Sanvey Gate, where, in a shop 7ft. 8in. high, 10ft. 6in. wide, and 40ft. in length, there were 16 stocking frames normally employing 19 persons. There were three small ventilators in the ceiling about 2½in. by 7in., and the Officer of Health reported: 'judging by the state of walls etc. I should say this shop has not been cleansed or limewashed for many years'.

The Surveyor suggested a shaft be constructed through the upper floor to the roof, necessitating the removal of one frame in the upper room. He suggested also more windows, but added 'it is doubtful if the men would have them open as they appear really averse to fresh air when at work'.[15]

The owner, a Mr. Weston, declared that he would not have any alterations made unless the Board paid his expenses. He was, however, informed that 'the Government have required the attention of the Board to be directed to the subject of ventilation of such buildings, and that they will be neglecting their duty if they do not require his compliance and that if he does not at once have the work done the Magistrates must have the matter placed in their hands'.[16] A further warning and limit of 14 days to comply with this seems to have been sufficient to induce co-operation.[17]

The Inspection of School Buildings

The Board was if anything more concerned about overcrowding of schools than of places of work. In this matter the initiative to remedial action seems to have come from Leicester, originating in Moore's report on three deaths from scarlet fever in 1857. He noted that the children all attended a school in Craven Street, where the room was only 12ft. by 9ft. and 8ft. high. In this room 25 to 30 children met daily. 'It is deeply to be regretted', observed Moore, 'that the Public Health Act gives no power to prevent this overcrowding in schools'.[18]

In October the following year Whetstone raised the issue again, and Moore was asked to report as to the number of cubic feet of space which, in his opinion, should be appropriated to each child.[19] In his report the Officer of Health noted several examples like the above of overcrowding in infant schools, and he digressed on the opinions of 'the celebrated Joseph Lancaster' as to the right cubic space of air for each child. Such authorities advised 130 to 180 cubic feet of 'atmospheric air' as the minimum allowable. But in a number of Leicester schools the figure was only 40 cubic feet. (That for one school he mentioned was only 26 cubic feet. The school was 10ft. by 10ft. and 8ft. high, with 31 children.) Moore recommended that in children's schools 'which are normally held in ordinary house rooms of about 8ft. high' a ground space of nine feet or 72 cubic feet of air be the recognised minimum.[20]

John Moore's introductory remarks to this report show clearly his adherence to the pythogenic theory: 'That the overcrowded state of many of these schools is injurious to the health of the children by causing them to breathe the same impure atmosphere again and again, cannot be doubted, and it if does not originate, it in many cases aggravates the diseases to which childhood is liable, and is probably the means of bringing many to a premature grave who might have lived to a good old age', he wrote. Effectively, of course, the remedy prescribed was the right one, whatever the faults of the diagnosis. Such overcrowded schools were a breeding ground of contagious disease and only good could result from limiting the numbers allowed to specific rooms, though it could be argued that there was some loss of educational provision as schools were closed in consequence of a bye-law which incorporated Moore's proposals. However, the educational value of these dame-schools was dubious to say the least. Dr. Chapman dismisses them as 'merely convenient arrangements for child minding'.[21]

In June 1860 the Inspector of Nuisances reported 'six people have discontinued keeping schools in consequence of the intention of the Board to enforce the byelaw'.[22] He presented a list of eight offenders, two of whom were to be sent letters of warning. The checking of these schools thereafter became a regular part of the Board's work.

Public schools were also obliged to observe the regulations as to ground space per pupil. There seems to have been some dispute as to the relevance of the height of rooms in calculating the air space per pupil. Alfred Burgess, the Chairman of the British Schools Committee pointed out that his schools were 'very lofty and well ventilated',[23] though they did not meet with the letter of the law in the ground area allotted to each pupil. He was told that the Committee could not 'allow the byelaw to be disregarded for any length of time'. Burgess reiterated: 'I cannot suppose that the byelaw means to limit the space allowed to each child, irrespective altogether of the height of the room: this would be very unreasonable. The rooms are well ventilated and we have never had any complaints'.[24] Pythogenic purism was surely on his side.

The Control of Pollution by Smoke

Attempts to control smoke itself began as early as 1842, when the Council set up a committee to study its abatement, seeking information from other industrial towns. The committee reported that practical means were available to effect the desired improvement and they felt confident that manufacturers would 'readily and cheerfully comply with the request of the Council in immediately directing the necessary alterations in the construction of their furnaces'.[25] They did not think bye-laws were necessary, but pointed out that in some boroughs offenders against smoke regulations were fined.

Repeated circulars to manufacturers urging them to take the necessary steps voluntarily, produced little or no effect and in June 1849 a bye-law made offenders liable to a penalty of £5, if the smoke in question was pronounced injurious to health by two medical practitioners.[26] The measure does not seem to have had much effect, however, and in 1856 a revised bye-law fixed the penalty at five shillings on any stoker and 40 shillings on the owner of offending chimneys.[27]

This revised measure was carried out in a reasonable and flexible manner; only chimneys seen to smoke for more than about 10 minutes normally led to prosecution. The exact time limit was not laid down, perhaps because of the strong reservations which some councillors had over the strict enforcement of this bye-law. When in 1859 Dr. Barclay led a public campaign against the smoke nuisance and several letters appeared in the press on the need for more stringent measures against pollution, Joseph Whetstone offered to resign his chairmanship rather than hinder the work of the Committee. He was, he said, the owner of several long chimneys in the town, and 'if it was the wish of the town that the bye-law should be carried out with greater severity than formerly . . . it would become a source of great annoyance to the trade and manufacturers of the town, and would be almost insupportable'.[28]

At this, other councillors joined in a chorus of support for Whetstone, the Mayor declaring that 'he did not believe any board in the kingdom executed its duties with greater fairness and impartiality'.[29] A close examination of the record suggests that Whetstone did sometimes find himself embarrassed by conflicting loyalties in this respect.[30] The consuming of smoke was not as easy as it had been originally supposed, and many manufacturers were genuinely perplexed as to how to satisfy the Board's requirements.

J. P. Clarke, a cotton reel manufacturer in New Walk and King Street, was obliged to dispose of large quantities of damp wood shavings upon his furnace. He threatened to close his works employing over 200 people if compelled to abandon the practice. He seems to have found a solution by advertising his chippings for sale as fuel.[31]

The Swimming Baths

J. P. Clarke had a penchant for utilising industrial waste. From early in the 1840s he had used the surplus hot water from his works to feed a private swimming bath about 40ft. long and 21ft. wide in New Walk. The Council agreed in 1847 to pay him £100 towards his expenses, and Clarke opened the baths to the public at one penny per person; this was to include the use of a clean towel.[32] In 1869, it was decided to take Clarke's baths entirely into the hands of the Corporation at a rent of £500 per year.[33] This arrangement enabled the Board to make special provision for the use of the baths. Thus in June 1870, it was decided: 'That the children from the Union be admitted to the Swimming Bath at one halfpenny each, they finding their own towels', and that 'the Baths be kept exclusively for females every Tuesday morning from eight to twelve o'clock, no male attendant to be on the premises . . .'.[34]

Within a few years J. P. Clarke was seeking an end to this agreement and the town was obliged to consider the erection of its own baths. A suitable site was found in Bath Lane near to the West Bridge. Once again the source of hot water was to be supplied by a local manufacturer, and the premises were designed to accommodate the expanding needs of the town, with two swimming baths for men and two for women, and 15 private slipper baths.

These plans were upset, however, by a combination of local parsimony and central government interference. It was rumoured that J. B. Everard's plans involved an expenditure of £20,000, and the local papers united in condemning this 'unwarrantable and wasteful expenditure'.[35] An enquiry by the Local Government Board resulted in the rejection of the scheme. Everard's revised plans left the women once again without separate accommodation, and the protracted debate deprived both sexes of any facilities for 18 months, as the New Walk premises had closed in December 1879 and the Bath Lane baths were not opened till July 1881.[36]

There were some who favoured a more spartan attitude and regarded interior swimming baths as an unwarranted use of public money. Extended facilities for outdoor bathing in the river would be, said James Thompson, a cheap and satisfactory alternative to such expenditure. It had long been the practice for men to bathe naked from the banks of the Soar, a custom which led to frequent protests from respectable citizens. Joseph Dare referred to 'the disgusting scenes tolerated in the Pasture, particularly in the bathing season',[37] while one citizen described the place as 'nothing else but a meeting place for all kinds of vice and filth'.[38] The Inspector of Nuisances, Joseph Wright, reported laconically that he found nothing to complain of.[39] He may have been less squeamish, or perhaps the word of his approach led to a rapid amelioration of behaviour.

The Inspector of Nuisances

To the humbler people of Leicester, Sergeant Wright must have been the very embodiment of the Corporation. It was he who reported on all manner of nuisances and misdemeanours such as throwing of stones and bowling of hoops by children, indecent exposure, or disgusting language, 'riding of velocipedes in New Walk', 'carpet shaking on the highway', or sale of offensive postcards. Peering in on backyards for offending pigsties, wagging a constabular finger at boys with catapults, timing the smoke from factory chimneys, and registering complaints about tripe boilers, gut cleaners and tallow chandlers, his presence must have symbolised authority as the point at which sanitarian ideals met the realities of urban living.

Wright already knew the townspeople intimately when he took George Bown's place. Eight years earlier he had led a party of three constables to deal with a riot at the workhouse and had been injured by a blow on the head from a stone.[40] He had joined the force in 1837 soon after its establishment and might well have risen to higher rank if he had not side-stepped into the field of public health. In 1860, he complained that his salary had not risen for 21 years, averaging with his fees as Summoning Officer for the Coroner, about £75 a year.[41] He pointed out that his duties had greatly expanded with the growth of the borough and that to his original work had been added the oversight of the night soil department, checking the water supplies and 'the carrying out of the Bye-laws respecting smoke nuisance, which requires exposure in all weathers'. The Highways and Sewage

Committee voted, however, that in their opinion, Wright was 'sufficiently remunerated for duties which he performs' and it refused his application.[42] Wright's basic pay came from the Watch Committee, and when in 1871 he persuaded them to raise it from 24s. to 30s. a week, the Highways Committee voted, with contemptible meanness, to reduce the sum it paid him 'by the amount of the addition made to his police pay'.[43] When Wright retired two years later, he was replaced by two other men, who each received £100 per annum.

This cavalier attitude to the Inspector of Nuisances was typical of other towns also. At Liverpool, so often in the forefront of sanitary progress, the Inspector 'received very little respect from the public and much less from his employers who usually treated him as an unskilled labourer'.[44] There was evidently a clear dividing line between the treatment of qualified staff who might command salaries commensurate with the earnings they could expect in private practice, such as the £1,000 paid to the Town Clerk in 1872 or the £700 paid to the Borough Surveyor in 1880, or the £500 given to the first full-time Medical Officer of Health, and the much lower rewards deemed appropriate for unskilled labourers among whom was the Inspector of Nuisances. Such relegation of key personnel to a lower status goes some way to explain the moves afoot in the late 19th century to lay down professional qualifications for the Inspectorate of Public Health.[45]

Chapter Five

INFANT MORTALITY

ONE OF THE PRINCIPAL weapons in the armoury of sanitary reformers prior to the passing of the Public Health Act had been Leicester's prominence in the list of death rates of major towns. In the first report of the Health of Towns Commission in 1845, Leicester's rate of 30 per 1,000 is exceeded only by Bristol (31), Manchester (32), and Liverpool (35). It was the hope of the reformers that mortality would diminish as the sewerage system came into operation and lessened the degree of atmospheric pollution.

To some extent their hope was realised. The crude death rate for Leicester fell substantially: by 1867 it was down to 24 per 1,000, while that of Liverpool remained at 30 and Manchester at 31 per 1,000. But what gave Leicester a grisly eminence in the national statistics was her appalling rate of infant mortality. While the rate for England and Wales fluctuated around 150 per 1,000 live births, that for Leicester rarely fell below 200, and in 1871 it actually reached the shattering figure of 252.4, or, in other words, that in that year more than one in four children died before their first birthday.[1]

As with general mortality rates, that of infants was always higher in towns than in rural districts. 'All diseases of infancy are heavier in the towns than the counties', wrote Dr. George Newman in his study of infant mortality in 1906, 'but immaturity is twice as fatal and epidemic diarrhoea seven times as fatal in the towns'.[2] Newman found immaturity or 'prematurity' to be the most common cause of deaths among infants. The precise nature of this condition was not clearly defined, however, and Newman disposed of this category with the remark that 'These children are simply born in such poor physical condition that they are unfit to live'.[3]

The second most common cause of death according to Newman was epidemic diarrhoea. Of this he says, 'Diarrhoeal diseases are ordinarily very much more fatal in urban districts than rural, are more dangerous to boys than to girls, and cause the greatest havoc among children in the first year of life, bringing about on an average one fifth of the total mortality of infants'.[4]

Leicester was not alone then in suffering this particular scourge, though the disease was more severe in Leicester than in most other towns, and it was especially virulent in the summer months of July, August and September. This led Dr. Crane, the Medical Officer of Health, to conclude that 'solar heat was to blame for the affliction', and he tried to show that Leicester suffered from a peculiarly humid atmosphere in summer.[5] Dr. Crane arrived at this conclusion after eliminating all the other popular explanations. Thus in 1873 he investigated the deaths from diarrhoea and found that they occurred just as frequently in houses which were 'airy' as in 'confined' ones, and more often in those which were described as in a 'good' sanitary state, with water supplied from the waterworks, than in insanitary houses with well water, and that the constitution of mother and father was by no means significant.[6] Crane's views excited considerable opposition from the public. A correspondent to the *Leicester Chronicle* wrote that Crane's heat theory was 'neither correct nor generally received'.[7] William Barfoot, a member of the Highways and Sewerage Committee, and later Mayor of Leicester, quoted a letter from 'a gentleman of very high scientific attainments' who wrote sarcastically suggesting that the Local Board of Health advertise for 'a square mile of awning to shade the town of Leicester from the sun's rays, and agree with the Waterworks Company to keep it constantly wet with streams of cool water from Bradgate'.[8]

Joseph Dare was not impressed with Crane's findings: 'There seems to be one fatal defect in these returns', he wrote, 'the Medical Officer, himself, did not examine into the cases individually, whether as regards the constitution of the persons, or their habitations'. Popular theory could not therefore be discounted on the basis of such investigations, and he argued that: 'where sickness and death appeared amidst seemingly healthful surroundings, there were hidden causes of death at work. These the Medical Officer himself should have tried to discover, and not leave us to infer, from data furnished by non-medical officials that light and air, space and cleanliness, motherly nurture and proper food, robust constitutions and mothers staying at home with their children, and, in short, what are called good sanitary conditions, show less favourably on the score of health than the reverse of these things'.[9]

A more thorough investigation was carried out in 1875 by two medical gentlemen, W. Elgar Buck and G. Cooper Franklin. They reported on the epidemic of 1874 and judged the disease to be specific to Leicester on account of its low-lying situation and imperfect drainage. Their report was a masterly summary of all the evidence for and against the various explanations advanced.

They rejected the view of Sir John Simon, the Medical Officer to the Privy Council, that the mortality was the result of neglect by women who went out to work. It was fashionable in middle-class Victorian society to decry the tendency for women to work in factories in the belief that they would neglect their wifely and motherly duties. The two doctors, however, found that three-quarters of the deaths occurred in homes where the mothers were at home and they declared firmly that: 'nursing mothers do not, as a rule neglect their children'.[10]

Buck and Franklin also rejected Simon's contention that poor nursing and the administering of opiates were responsible, though they viewed it as 'a matter of deep concern that there should be no restraint whatever as [to] the amount of "dosing" an infant may receive at the hands of its nurse'.[11] They made close examination of the domestic circumstances in which the deaths had occurred, to test the common assumption that overcrowding, neglect and insanitary conditions were to blame. But neither did they find support for such a view. 'When we come to point out that this summer disease is not so fatal among the very poor, it is almost unknown in many of the most over-crowded courts in the town, and that, as a rule, general insanitary conditions do not exist, then', said they, 'the explanation is not so easy, and that there are other factors at work, other peculiarities affecting the working population, or the town in which they live'.[12]

They pointed out that in general Leicester was a most healthy place: 'It stands pre-eminently', they said, 'in comparison with other large towns in respect of the width of its streets, the absence of cellar dwellings, the comparative freedom from crowded courts, and houses built back-to-back'. After noting that as a rule 'the denser the population the poorer it is', they observe that in the most crowded parts of the town 'curiously enough, this specific diarrhoea is not found'. Thus they conclude that 'this disease does not follow upon poverty any more than it does upon density'.[13]

They disposed of the notion that the water from Thornton and Cropston reservoirs was at fault, but then turned to Wicksteed's sewerage system which they criticised most heavily. Sewage-contaminated soil was indeed one of the contributing factors which Buck and Franklin believed to be responsible for the disease in Leicester. Added to this, many of the houses built at the time were on made-up ground in former clay-pits. Buck and Franklin examined some such building sites and found clay being dug at one end, while houses were being built at the other; and in between the two operations all kinds of rubbish were thrown in to make up the ground. In one example of such made-up ground they found a heap 'about six yards square, specially foul; consisting of wet ashbin refuse, rabbit skins alive with maggots, cabbage and other vegetable refuse, lemons, rope, turnips'.[14]

They finally reverted to Crane's heat theory. The doctors considered that 'heat, in conjunction with a water-logged soil, forms a favourable condition for the production of epidemic diarrhoea in Leicester'.[15] They recommended that the subsoil be drained of superfluous water; a free outfall be found for the sewers of the town and that clay-pits or other excavations should not be filled up with filthy ashbin refuse and then built upon.

In fact the rate of infant mortality and the incidence of weanling or summer diarrhoea was very high in the country as a whole, not falling substantially until the turn of the century. The national phenomenon was investigated in the late 19th century by several eminent medical authorities. Dr. Ballard reported on the causes of summer diarrhoea to the Local Government Board in 1889 and concluded that 'infants fed from the breast are remarkably exempt from diarrhoea as compared with infants that have been fed otherwise: and that feeding from "the bottle" had been principally concerned in the fatal diarrhoea of infants'.[16]

As it happened, Buck and Franklin found striking evidence to suggest this, but they seem to have been curiously blind to its significance. They found in fact that only 10 per cent. of the infants who died were wholly breastfed.[17] Perhaps they hesitated to lay emphasis on this finding because it conflicted with reports of other investigations carried out by Dr. Crane and by William Johnston, his assistant, in 1878.[18] Johnston found 69.3 per cent. of the fatal cases had been suckled, against 30.7 per cent. bottle-fed or fed on a mixed diet. This he regarded as 'a good refutation of the theory that "hand feeding" is the chief factor in the causation of the disease'.[19] However, it is impossible to know exactly what is meant by 'suckled'–did this refer to the first few months of life or the entire life span of the infant? The crucial period was the time of weaning away from breast milk when a child might reject other food and develop diarrhoea. The period of weaning presented two main dangers: that of infection from the use of contaminated utensils or unclean food, and the danger that improper foods might be rejected by the child's stomach. It is important to bear in mind that diarrhoea is not (strictly speaking) a disease but a condition. It is caused by infection of the alimentary canal, conveyed by food. The infant stomach cannot accept such infected food, which sets up irritation in the intestines and remains undigested.

Breast-fed babies are virtually immune from such dangers since their mothers' milk is the most natural and balanced diet possible. But infants weaned off the breast, at a time of the year when bacteria multiply most rapidly, suffer acute risk of infection. This explains why Crane found a significant correlation between the temperature and summer diarrhoea. Sustained high temperature favours the growth of bacteria, especially in milk. George Newman, writing in 1906, said: 'Unclean milk is almost a solution of bacteria and little short of rank poison to an infant'.[20]

The much higher mortality which Victorian investigators noted in urban districts resulted from the greater length of time which toxic bacteria had to develop in milk. Newman showed that epidemic diarrhoea was seven times as fatal in the towns as in country districts.

It might be thought that pure cow's milk would provide a perfect substitute for human milk, but the composition of milk for each species is different according to its different needs. The cow has four stomachs to the human being's single one, and the milk of the cow is less easily digested by a human infant. Human and cow's milk contain about equal quantities of water and fat, but whereas cow's milk contains 3.5 per cent. protein, that of a woman contains only 1.5 per cent., and while human milk contains 6.5 per cent. sugar, the milk of the cow contains only 4.5 per cent. Cow's milk also has a higher caseinogenic content (i.e., the cheese-producing element) so that it has a curd which is too hard for the infant human being to digest easily.[21]

The content of modern artificial milk for babies is, of course, adjusted to resemble that of mother's milk, by increasing the sugar content relative to protein and adding other ingredients, but this was not so until the very late 19th century. One of the contributory factors in the decline of infant mortality was the improvement in the quality of milk sold. This was in part the result of systematic sampling by public analysts and the subsequent action by magistrates against those found guilty of adulterating milk.

There were in the closing years of the 19th century depots established for the distribution of sterilised milk, especially prepared for infants, such as that set up in St. Helens in 1899. But it was not until 1906 that a milk depot was opened in Leicester.[22] The dramatic fall in infant mortality since 1900 is almost certainly a reflection of these improvements in the quality of milk fed to babies. The question remains, however, why Leicester should have been so particularly vulnerable. It seems possible that Crane's heat theory was not entirely wide of the mark. Leicester does enjoy, or rather suffer, a peculiarly humid atmosphere in the summer months which may be explained by its situation in the valley of the River Soar, with the Charnwood Hills on one side and the East Leicestershire uplands to the other. It could be that this local climate favoured the spread of intestinal infections as well as the curdling of cow's milk. There is no doubt that the disease was most marked at the end of the summer season and was most virulent when the temperature rose above normal for the time of the year. This was the season when flies would be most active in carrying infection, and when bacteria associated with some forms of enteritis would spread most rapidly, particularly in soil contaminated with sewage.

Joseph Gordon's relaying of the sewers, together with the spread of such practices as the sterilisation of feeding bottles, the wider use of soaps and disinfectants and the general improvement of nutritional standards all contributed to the eventual decline of infant mortality. In 1905, Dr. C. Killick Millard, the Medical Officer of Health for Leicester, was able to record a rate of 146.5, the lowest since 1860, and apart from isolated rises in 1906 and 1915 the rate continued to tumble downwards thereafter. With good reason, Dr. Millard boasted that 'what was at one time the great blot on the sanitary statistics of the town, viz. the excessive infant mortality, is being wiped away'.[23]

Smallpox and Vaccination

Leicester's peculiar susceptibility to summer diarrhoea in infants was an affliction for which, in the existing state of knowledge, it could hardly be held culpable. The Corporation through its health officers conducted many enquiries and did all that medical experts advised to alleviate the scourge. By contrast, in the matter of smallpox, the people of

Leicester seem to have courted notoriety and deliberately flouted medical orthodoxy.

Smallpox was one of the most dreaded diseases of the early 19th century, though in fact its incidence was declining in one of those long-run trends that bring no comfort to the actual sufferer. One factor in diminishing the effect of the disease was the spread of innoculation in the 18th century, and of vaccination in the 19th century. Jenner's use of cowpox to protect human beings from the scourge of smallpox meant that there was much less risk of contracting the disease as a result of preventive innoculation, and by 1840 the older method was proscribed by law while vaccination was officially encouraged. In 1853 it became compulsory and further Acts endeavoured to secure its universal application.[24]

There was always an undercurrent of hostility to the practice. William Gardiner recalled the suspicion popularly entertained toward vaccination when Jenner made his experiments: 'I well remember the noise the discovery made . . . The windows of booksellers were filled with pictures of men and women with horns growing out of their heads, and features transformed into those of horned cattle'.[25]

With progressive attempts to enforce the practice, this hostility to vaccination increased. The 'cat and mouse' Act of 1867 allowed magistrates to fine and imprison parents for not having their children vaccinated, and furthermore empowered them to punish defaulters continuously until the original offence was put right. The injustice and inhumanity of this provision resulted in the foundation of the Anti-Vaccination League, whose spearhead in the campaign against enforcement was in Leicester.

Opponents of the practice gained much support in Leicester as a result of the imprisonment in 1871 of Mrs. Wrigley, who was the widow of a local doctor, and refused to have her children vaccinated. She appears to have 'courted martyrdom' by writing to the mayor informing him that she could not obey the law, whereupon she was kept in custody for two hours.[26]

There followed a protracted correspondence in the *Chronicle* between William Lakin, who signed himself

'M.D. (U.S.)' or 'botanic practitioner' (i.e., a homeopath) and a 'public vaccinator'. 'Cannot the medical man see', wrote Lakin, 'that the system of Jenner is an utter failure, that more disease and death is produced through its adoption than by smallpox in its natural form and with proper treatment'.[27]

The 'public vaccinator' replied that most of the faults ascribed to vaccination were traceable to carelessness on the part of parents, or to faulty procedure by inexpert vaccinators.[28] There is little doubt that some practitioners of the operation were quite unqualified to perform it. Sir John Simon confessed himself 'shocked, utterly shocked' that 'hitherto no security had been taken that the vaccination so universally offered and so extensively enforced should be useful or even harmless to the recipient'[29] and he set about establishing a national system of training and examination for vaccinators.

Despite Simon's efforts, mistakes sometimes occurred and were well-publicised by the anti-vaccinators. Lakin made a great deal of the findings of Jonathan Hutchinson, F.R.C.S., who investigated a case in 1871, in which 11 out of 13 vaccinated adults developed a mild form of syphilis.[30] Hutchinson was a firm supporter of compulsory vaccination and the greatest living authority on syphilis. As a result of this investigation, he urged that vaccination should no longer be performed using the lymph (i.e. the vesicular matter) taken from infected children, but only with that taken direct from a calf. In this way it would not be possible for hereditary diseases such as syphilis to be passed on to patients through the lymph taken from infected infants. It was not until 1898, however, that arm-to-arm vaccination was legally prohibited.[31]

The balance of statistical evidence favoured the vaccinators, although the emotive strength of their propaganda was soon outstripped by that of the Anti-Vaccination League, so far as Leicester was concerned. The Local Board maintained official support for the policy of vaccination but looked also to other measures in order to combat the disease. One of the most important elements in their strategy was the building in 1866 of a disinfecting chamber where the public could have all bedding, linen and clothing which might be contaminated, disinfected free of charge. The Board also provided a suitable conveyance for carrying articles to the chamber and another for use after the disinfection had been carried out.[32]

The medical officer was asked to issue handbills giving information as to disinfection of clothes and the benefits of vaccination, and the attendants at the Public Baths were instructed to refuse admission to sufferers from smallpox.[33] In the same month, May 1872, there was a house-to-house inspection ordered of the entire town to discover cases needing sanitary attention, such as privies and cesspools which might give rise to disease.[44]

A more positive step was the setting up of an isolation hospital. The idea was proposed by Wyatt Crane in his report of 1867. It was opened in 1871 on land known as Freake's ground to the north-west of the town and outside its boundaries. Prior to this, emergency accommodation was found in Soar Lane near to the Friends' Meeting House.[35] Prudently, the local Quakers rented alternative premises for the time being.

The policy of immediate isolation of sufferers and strenuous efforts to maintain cleanliness in all parts of the town coupled with a virtual abandonment of compulsory vaccination came to be known as the 'Leicester system'. The town's freedom from smallpox for many years seemed to confirm the wisdom of the system, and even in 1934 the retiring Medical Officer of Health, Dr. Millard, declared that 'infant vaccination is not now necessary for the protection of the community'.[36]

The driving force in the campaign against compulsory vaccination in Leicester was J. T. Biggs, a Sanitary and Waterworks engineer, who became secretary of the Leicester Anti-Vaccination movement in 1869. He was a member of the Board of Guardians and a Conservative councillor on the Sanitary Committee from 1888 to 1910. He castigated vaccination as 'blood polluting quackery' and organised a highly successful campaign against its supporters. Thus at a meeting in 1873 the audience was urged 'not to vote for any man either for local or imperial offices, who did not go in for anti-vaccination'.[37] In his book, *Sanitation Versus Vaccination,* Biggs wrote that 'Penal compulsion in a matter so closely affecting the tenderest and deepest feelings of parents was regarded as a poll tax, of an even more obnoxious character than that which occasioned the uprising in 1381, since its effect was not only to be felt in every household and in every family, but a risky surgical operation was super-added, and ordained by law to be inflicted upon all children born into the world!'[38]

Biggs, who led and inspired the movement against the Vaccination Acts, was a fanatic who believed in his cause with absolute conviction. The account he gives of the movement in Leicester reads like the story of a revivalist crusade. It is perhaps significant that he was a Conservative in his politics, for the anti-vaccination cause was one which might appeal to the electorate across traditional party allegiance, and it is clear that Biggs used the vaccination issue as a weapon against his political opponents.

At the local election of 1882, both Liberals lost their seats in East St. Margaret's Ward to the two Conservative anti-vaccinators. A contemporary poster appealed to Liberals to defect on this issue: 'There is no political crisis in this for the Liberal party', it said, 'if they lose the seats, they still retain their great majority in the Council. If ever there was a time when Liberal anti-vaccinators should lay aside party for principle it is now'.[39]

A well-known Tory, H. D. Dudgeon, wrote to the *Leicester Daily Post* in the emotive language typical of the movement: 'In the choice of Town Councillors we neither want masters to ride rough shod over us nor non-descripts to sit in meek silence while the child is torn from the mother's breast and vaccinated by force before her eyes, as is now openly threatened by our exasperated antagonists'.[40]

However, there were prominent Liberals in the campaign; in particular, P. A. Taylor, who sat as one of the town Members of Parliament from 1862 to 1884.[41] He at one time supported compulsion, but changed his views and became President of the London Society for the Abolition of Compulsory Vaccination.

If the movement resembled a religious campaign, it also had its 'martyrs', for no less than 2,274 summonses were issued in Leicester between 1883 and 1886 for failure to present children for vaccination. The success of the movement can be judged from the figures for vaccination, 'whereas in 1867 over 94 per cent. of the children born were vaccinated, in 1897 only 1.3 per cent.' underwent the operation.[42]

The measures advocated by the Anti-Vaccination League depended to a great extent upon prompt isolation and segregation of smallpox cases, and quarantine for all who had been in contact with them. Dr. Johnston, when Medical Officer, persuaded the Corporation to obtain a Local Act, in 1879, which made notification of infectious diseases compulsory.[43] Another important development in preventive medicine was the institution of health visitors.

The visiting of poor families by middle-class ladies bent on offering good advice and moral uplift was a familiar feature in Victorian life as in its literature. The credit for conducting such visits in order to foster practical knowledge of hygiene and health precautions seems to belong to the Manchester and Salford Ladies' Sanitary Association[44] founded in 1862, whose activities led to the appointment of the first professional health visitors by Manchester Corporation in 1890. Leicester's appointment of Mrs. Hartshorn as 'female inspector' to 'go round to the inhabitants of the courts and impress on them the value of cleanliness' in October 1895 was probably the earliest example of an official health visitor apart from that of Manchester.

In 1896 Mrs. Hartshorn was reported to have visited over 6,000 homes with a consequent improvement in their cleanliness. Hygiene became a matter of personal pride, and conditions improved 'solely from the reason that the inhabitants strongly object to having their houses found in a state of filth, time after time, when visited'.[45]

The actual operation of the Vaccination Acts was the responsibility of the Boards of Guardians who were required to appoint a vaccination officer. The remuneration of this officer was in part dependent on the volume of his work, so that in Leicester he found himself considerably worse off as antipathy to vaccination increased. The Guardians were not permitted to pay him a fixed salary and there was an annual battle with the Local Government Board over the supplementation of his income. Eventually, when the vaccinator retired in 1898, the Guardians refused to appoint a successor, since only a tenth of the parents obtained certificates of exemption and only one per cent. of the children in Leicester were vaccinated. There seemed little point in paying a salaried officer simply in order to bring fruitless prosecutions.[46]

The Local Government Board, however, proceeded to issue a writ against the 45 Guardians who refused to vote for such an appointment, and when the Guardians attempted to evade the law by appointing a known anti-vaccinator, he was disqualified by the authorities in London. The dispute ended with the Leicester Board being compelled to appoint another officer who gave a solemn assurance that he would, if need be, defy them. The sledgehammer of authority was thus used quite deliberately to crush this residue of local resistance to vaccination, and the Guardians had to pay a bill of £1,220 15s. 8d. in legal costs. 'A great community', wrote the *Leicester Chronicle,* 'is now to be worried in order to gratify an aggressive department and satisfy a stupid statute'.[47]

Seen from London, of course, the intransigence of Leicester was a wilful refusal to face scientific facts. The lives of children were being set at risk through the obtuse bigotry of a few provincial cranks. Both sides quoted figures to suit their predetermined views. If the balance of statistical evidence favoured vaccination, there was ample evidence to show that it was not as effective as the authorities tried to pretend. It is perhaps not quite irrelevant to note that in 1973 the government decided to end vaccination against smallpox because treating all children would entail risks from the operation itself, greater than the statistical probability of deaths from smallpox in unvaccinated children.[48]

A direct consequence of the vaccination controversy was a relaxation of compulsion by the central government and the adumbration of an important principle of the British political system, namely, the right of conscientious objection. For as a result of the determined resistance to compulsory vaccination, especially in Leicester, parents were given the right in 1898 to obtain certificates of exemption. Even in 1934 when Dr. Millard retired there were only 98 vaccinations in Leicester and 3,438 certificates of exemption recorded.[49]

Had there been a serious epidemic of smallpox in the town, the anti-vaccinators might have met with less credulity; but in fact Leicester never suffered such an epidemic and, as no one could attribute its immunity to vaccination, the treatment was regarded as superfluous. Instead, Leicester put its trust in a rigorous policy of public cleansing, together with stringent measures of isolation and quarantine. Careful attention to cleaning the streets, the removal of health hazards, and the erection of public incinerators for the removal of rubbish were the essence of the 'Leicester system' or 'Leicester method'. Insofar as the local death rate from smallpox was lower than that for the country at large, the Leicester method justified itself, but it is probable that it succeeded in part because vaccination elsewhere reduced the likelihood of infection spreading to Leicester.

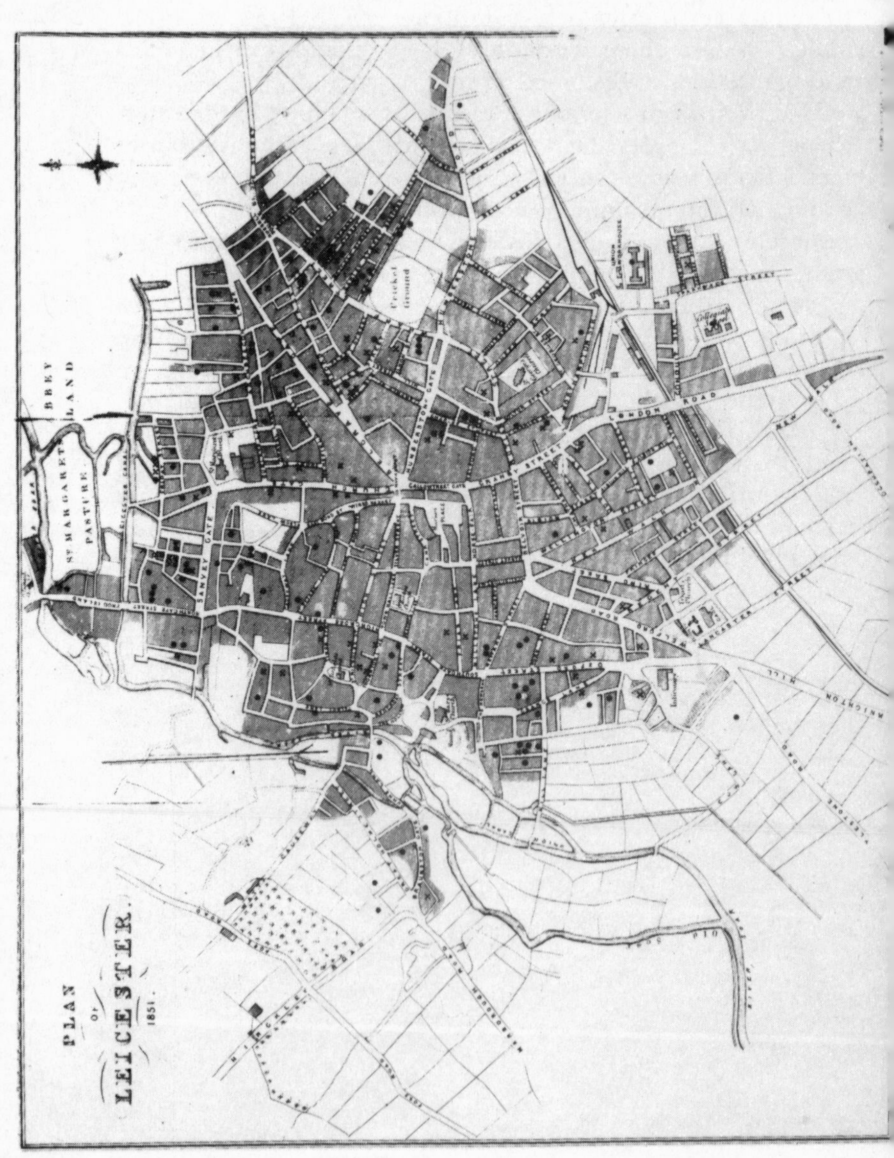
PLAN
OF
LEICESTER.
1851.
St. MARGARET'S
PASTURE
Cricket
Ground
SANVEY GATE
HUMBERSTONE GATE
LONDON ROAD
Infirmary

Chapter Six

SOMEWHERE TO LIVE

ONE OF THE CONSEQUENCES of urban expansion was the rise in land values in town centres and the crowding of more and more people into these areas. Poor housing conditions are often explained in terms of profiteering landlords and speculative builders, but given the economic facts of low wages and a competitive demand for land–it might be used for shops, offices, roads, railway stations, and a dozen other purposes as well as house building–the rents that working men could afford would not obtain more than two or three rooms within doors and a derisory yard without.

London, Glasgow, Manchester and other large towns exhibited the results of such economic pressures in the notorious slums depicted by Dickens, Engels, and Mayhew. But in this matter Leicester was fortunate. It was small enough for its citizens to remain within walking distance of green fields, and it never suffered from legal obstacles to development inflicted on places like Nottingham and Coventry.

There was, therefore, as has already been indicated, an abundance of land available for building purposes adjoining the borough. It is true that the same economic pressures applied within the town as elsewhere–low wages and a competitive demand for land in the neighbourhood of business–and these pressures did lead to some overcrowding, but what is remarkable in Leicester is that there was so little congestion even during the decades of most rapid population increase. The census figures illustrate this relative spaciousness of Leicester. If we compare the total population with the number of houses available in 1871, we find a density per house of 4.8; considerably lower than that for the country as a whole, namely 5.6 for the United Kingdom and 5.4 for England.[1] Figures such as these are extremely crude, however, since they do not indicate the number of rooms per house, or tell us anything about the standard of accommodation. A somewhat more accurate measure is that which relates to the number of persons per room, though the statistics are not available till later in the century.

E. R. Dewsnup, using the census figures for 1901, listed 84 County Boroughs in England and Wales with populations over 50,000, showing that Leicester had the lowest percentage of population living in overcrowded tenements, i.e., with more than two persons per room, with the exception of Northampton and Bournemouth.[2] The percentage figures were 1.04 for Leicester and 0.97 for Northampton, and 0.62 for Bournemouth; as against, for example, 3.65 for Nottingham, 10.38 for Birmingham, and 34.54 for Gateshead. Thus, when the age of Victoria drew to its close, despite the existence of pockets of slums in the older parts of the town, the people of Leicester enjoyed more spacious accommodation than the vast majority of their contemporaries.

Half a century earlier the slums were much more in evidence, and the contrast between their squalid appearance and that of the town as a whole did not escape the notice of official observers. Ranald Martin, in his report of 1845 for the Health of Towns Commission, noted Leicester's low density of population, which arose, he said, 'from the numerous gardens everywhere to be found'. But he commented also on the 'low, ill-ventilated and badly lighted' houses in the poorer parts of the town.[3] Four years later William Ranger likewise remarked, 'the worst houses are to be found in the older quarters of the town; they are the habitations of the working classes and the poor, and are faulty both in arrangement and structure'; for example, he found instances in Red Cross Street, near the old town centre, 'where a man, wife, and eleven children [were] occupying one room 11 feet 6 inches by 10 feet 9 inches, by 6 feet 9 inches high'. He cited also eleven houses in Porkshop Yard, off Abbey Street, which were literally converted pigsties of one room each, measuring 14 feet by 10 feet and 6½ feet high, containing on average five persons per house. Ranger learned that it was customary for the relieving officer of the Poor Law to provide shelter for the destitute in this same yard. 'At one end of this yard there is a large house let in separate apartments, which, like the common lodging houses, is a nest of fever and disease. The relieving officer makes use of these lodging houses for lodging the casual paupers'.[4]

Despite such grim revelations, Ranger adjudged these cases to form 'the exception rather than the rule'. Leicester was virtually ignored by Chadwick in his great report of 1842, for there was little in the town to compare with the shocking conditions existing in Manchester, Liverpool, Nottingham and in the metropolis.

In the late 1840s, then, the standard of housing in Leicester was probably a good deal better than average. The fact that it remained so, despite rapid growth in the population, is certainly due in part to the enlightened attitude of the local authority. The Council made no attempt to control such standards until the foundation of the Local Board of Health in 1849. From that time the regulations devised by the Leicester authorities were gradually strengthened and consistently enforced.

Here we must take issue with the view of Professor Simmons, who in his book *Leicester Past and Present,* seems determined to belittle the achievement of the reformed Corporation by stating that the worst slums were erected during the very years when the Board of Health was actively engaged in promoting improved standards.

Back-to-Backs In Leicester

According to Professor Simmons the town 'contained no back-to-back houses' in the '40s, while in the '60s and '70s they were numerous. Of the Local Board Professor Simmons says its 'intentions were good. But it proved impossible to realise them in practice'.[5] He ascribes such failure to the timidity of the Council in failing to use its full powers. If it were true, as Professor Simmons argues, that Leicester had no back-to-backs in the 1840s, then one would not object

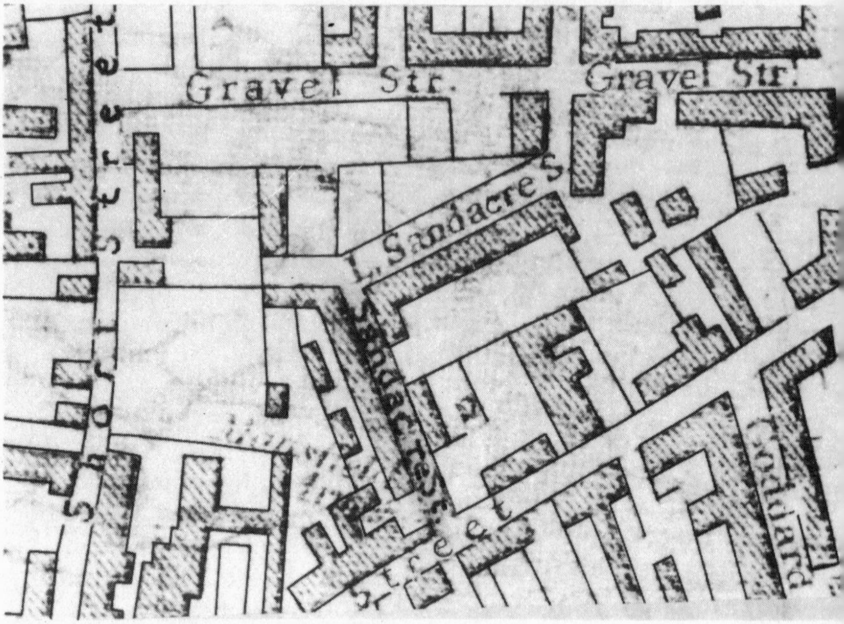

Fig. 5. Lower Sandacre Street on map of 1840

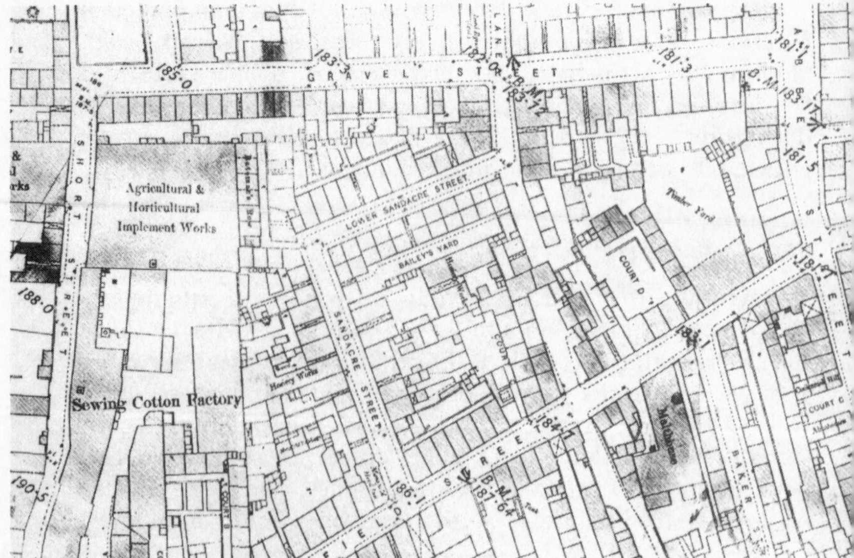

Fig. 6. Lower Sandacre Street on map of 1885

to his strictures on the competence of the Local Board, but the balance of available evidence suggests that the vast majority of such back-to-backs were erected during the years before the Public Health Act of 1848 came into operation.

A close examination of the town map of 1840 (part of which is reproduced opposite) suggests the existence of some back-to-backs which can still be found on the large-scale Ordnance Survey sheets of the 1880s. There are difficulties in defining precisely what is meant by back-to-backs. A free-standing hovel with no back door or windows would not technically fall within the category, but the distinction between such a hovel and one actually constructed with its rear wall common to another dwelling is one of more interest to the academic historian than to the unfortunate inhabitant of either, for in neither could air circulate freely.

If we take a broad definition of back-to-backs as 'houses without rear doors or windows' then we may yet find the odd example of such a construction standing in Leicester and dating from long before the 1840s, when, according to Professor Simmons, they did not exist. One such extant example is Cramant's Yard in King Street, which dates from the 1820s. The Ordnance Survey map of 1885, reproduced as Pl. 19, shows the layout of the yard in which, according to the census of 1841, there lived 22 people apart from Hannah Cramant, 'schoolmistress', and her five children on King Street itself.

It was not initially within the competence of the Local Board to forbid the building of houses simply because they were constructed on the back-to-back principle, but the officer of health urged the propriety of extending the bye-laws in this respect as early as 1851. The influential and respected town missionary, Joseph Dare, repeatedly drew attention to the evils of houses without back doors or windows, estimating in 1865 that there were 'at least 1,500 in this town', with 'between seven and eight thousand sweltering in these wretched unhealthy abodes'.[6]

It is probable that these dwelling houses were in the older parts of the town, built before the establishment of the

Board of Health or during its early years, for such houses would not have received the approval of the Board after 1859 and it is very unlikely that they would have been built without the Board's knowledge. In another report two years later, Dare gives us a vivid description of living conditions in such houses: 'In a house in a close back yard, with one up and one down floor room, a father and mother, six children, some of them sixteen or seventeen years of age, and a grown up young man herded together. Three of the children have had fever, and the youth has been in the Infirmary, in consumption. Fever, more or less severe, has frequently appeared in this household'.[7] Dare suggests that landlords were partly to blame for this sort of situation: 'I asked the father', he says, 'why he did not go to a larger house? He said he had tried to obtain one, but landlords will not let property where there are families. To make matters worse there were actually two or three hens sitting under the stairs—so this dirty confined space serves for coal hole, pantry and fowl pen . . . In another case the father of the family was taken to the fever house and died. The wife thought, very properly that the house should be well cleaned, as it had not been white-washed for seven years. But the house agent peremptorily refused to have it done, and threatened her with immediate expulsion if she made any to do about it . . . Landlords who often reside at a distance, are unacquainted with such circumstances, and others, who are needy and penurious, wink at them'.[8]

Following the Public Health Act of 1858 with its adoptive clauses on control of new buildings, the regulations of the Leicester Board were codified with additions and, in 1859, formed part of the town's bye-laws. It was then stipulated that a minimum space of 150 square feet had to be left at the side or rear of each house, and the depth of this yard was to increase with the addition of a third storey. The minimum height of ceilings was fixed at 8ft. 6ins. for ground floor and basement rooms, and 8ft. for others. The 1858 regulations also stipulated that one room on each floor should have a minimum of 108 sq. ft. of floor space. The size of windows was laid down, insofar as one window in each room had to measure at least one-tenth of the floor area. Also in 1859, it was laid down that the height of new buildings should not exceed the width of the streets.[9]

These regulations were not particularly stringent, but they were effectively applied to all new buildings, factories, workshops and to the villas of the rich as well as to the houses of the poor. In Nottingham, by contrast, there were most enlightened criteria for the observance of builders which seem very largely to have been ignored. Thus, Dr. Chapman notes that regulations issued by Nottingham Council for private dwelling houses under the Enclosure Act of 1845 stated that they were not to adjoin others on more than two sides; they should have yards of at least 30 sq. ft.; three bedrooms, a lavatory, dustpit, water supply, and nine-inch walls. But these regulations were apparently too exacting for the builders of low-priced dwellings, and they appear to have been openly flouted.[10]

Liverpool took the lead in laying down standards for the observation of private builders under its Local Act of 1842, which said that no courts should be built unless 15 feet wide and open at one end; that new houses had to have one room at least 100 feet square; and all but garret rooms were to be eight feet high. Such regulations, however, again tended to put new houses beyond the reach of many of the poor, especially the Irish immigrants, so that pressure on existing housing became even greater. Duncan, the Medical Officer of Health, had to advise the Council not to pursue so rapidly the policy of closing occupied cellars.[11]

In Leeds the Council continued to allow the erection of back-to-backs until 1937, despite the fact that they had been made illegal in 1909.[12]

In Leicester, by contrast, the Board of Health effectively enforced its minimum standards and, for the most part, builders observed standards above the Board's criteria. The strict observance of the Board's regulations was effected by careful surveillance from the outset. Offenders were summoned to appear before the Board, or rather the Highways and Sewerage Committee, and were warned that the magistrates would act if necessary. In practice this was very rarely necessary, the threat being enough to secure compliance.[13]

The Leicester Freehold Land Society

The limitations of the powers of the Local Board were dramatically exposed by a case which arose in 1853, involving a builder who had acquired two plots of land on the Humberstone Road estate of the Freehold Land Society.

The Freehold Land Society was founded in 1849, modelled on that of Birmingham. The object was to purchase land at wholesale prices with the money contributed by members in the form of shares, the land being distributed among those who were lucky in a draw for allotments. Members paid three shillings fortnightly for each share of £50 and were at liberty to take up their lots either through outright purchase or by mortgaging their land at 5 per cent. with the Society. When the land was secured, money still had to be found to build on it. Often, therefore, the lots were sold to private speculators and builders.

The Freehold Land Society included on its board all the most influential figures of the local ruling establishment. Richard Harris and John Ellis, the town's two Members of Parliament, were its patrons; and associated with it were Joseph Whetstone, the Biggs brothers, James Thompson of the *Chronicle*, and many others who were, or later became, among the most prominent figures in Leicester. Its president, John Biggs, addressing the inaugural meeting of the Society in 1849, proclaimed that its object was 'to overthrow the Tory domination in the county'[14] by gaining for each shareholder an income from land of 40 shillings per year, so entitling him to a freehold county vote.

So far as its political ambition was concerned, it probably had a very limited success, for there was no means of ensuring that the newly enfranchised would vote against the Tories. The *Leicester Journal* saw this more clearly than its radical opponents, anticipating that property ownership would tend to produce political conservatives. 'For once', it said, 'these liberty mongers have overstepped the mark; . . . We shall be delighted to see the day when the working man shall have become an independent freeholder–independent, not as Radicalism construes independence, viz., captives dragged at the chariot wheels of their stern, uncompromising, unforgiving Radical tyrants; but independent of everything and everybody but right principle. Then, will these disturbers have "done some service to the state", by making her sons good citizens . . . conservators of . . . that Constitution under which they have become freeholders, and have obtained a stake in the country's weal, and which they will be too wise to peril merely to pleasure to a parasite or pander to a pimp'.[15]

Whatever the long-term effects of wider land ownership, the immediate potentialities of the situation were not lost on some of the less scrupulous buyers of the Society's land. The Humberstone Road estate comprised streets appropriately named Cobden Street, Bright Street and Freehold Street, as well as those named after Curzon and Stanley. The Society had not thought it necessary to place any restrictions on the use of plots taken up by its members, and it was common practice for such allotments to be resold.

In 1852 the Society's own solicitor and his clerk each sold a plot of land in Curzon Street to a Mr. Thomas Bland, who at once prepared to build 11 houses on the space intended for two.[16]

It was not, however, until June 1853 that the Society awakened to the danger of what was happening. At this juncture, John Biggs as President, Edward Shipley Ellis as Trustee, and John D. Harris as Vice-President, with 26 other persons, signed a memorial to the Local Board. They appealed to the Board to prevent the erection of the property 'so crowded together and inferior in quality as to be highly detrimental to the surrounding property'.[17] In view of the impression sometimes given that the sole object of such societies was to obtain the county franchise, it is worth noting the views presented in this memorial. The petitioners argued: 'That the Society have been desirous to pay out the land they have purchased in such a manner as to be most conducive to the public health and the social improvement of those who had the privilege of allotments and might be desirous of building either for occupation or investment'.[18] They stated that the streets had been laid out 30 feet wide and that 'they have also expended upwards of £1,300 in draining, in the construction and paving of the streets so as to make them as airy and healthful and respectable as possible'. There was also room for good gardens and ample space around properties so that they might be 'highly agreeable and healthy residences'.

The memorial further pointed out that many members built houses which they would not have built had they supposed that buildings such as those planned by Mr. Bland would be erected. They assured the Board that

> It was never supposed that the allotments would be purchased from the allotees for the purpose of being crowded with courts and small houses, yielding possibly a profitable return for a time to the builder, but highly detrimental to the health and morals of the neighbourhood and frustrating entirely the design of the members, viz. to introduce a healthier and better description of houses for working men at an equal or less cost than could be obtained in the centre of the town.

They feared that 'other builders . . . will imitate the plans of Mr. Bland and make them even more objectionable if the Board suffers the plans in question to be adopted'.[19]

Following the presentation of this memorial, Bland attended a meeting of the Highways and Sewerage Committee and was asked to curtail the number of houses he proposed to erect. On 31 August, however, a further memorial was received from 29 inhabitants and owners of property in the neighbourhood of Curzon Street, who claimed that 'the foundations have now been laid for several miserable hovels in the background, and that the number of houses will be as great and the plan upon which they are to be built tenfold more objectionable than we at first supposed possible'. They declared

> That the plans upon which these houses are being built is filthy and sets common decency at defiance; the houses have only one door and that in front, so that all the filth, dung, refuse etc. that is made in each house must be brought out in the presence of all the neighbourhood and taken to a cluster of privies . . . close to the front door . . . or it must remain in the house breeding fever and malaria on a scale never surpassed in the most horrible

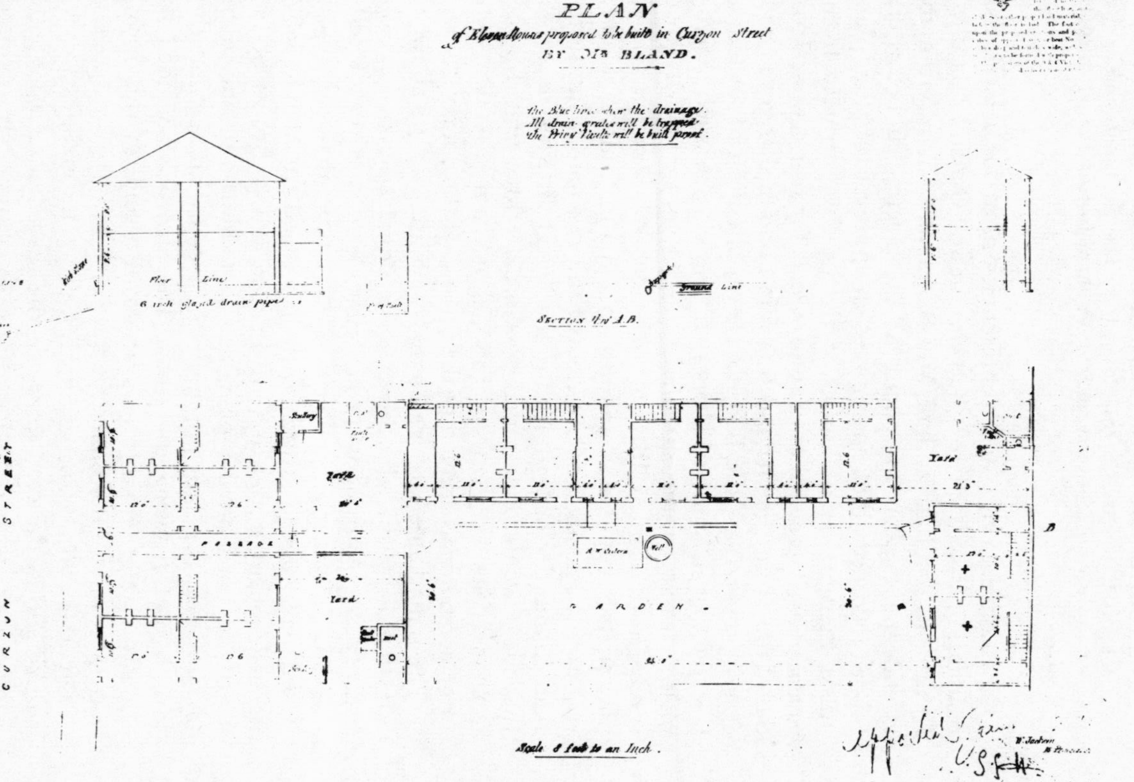

Fig. 7. Mr. Bland's original plan for eleven houses in Curzon Street

> dens that London or Liverpool contained in the days when Sanitary Boards had no existence and avaricious men were allowed to prejudice the public health and degrade the poor to their hearts' content . . . The houses would be unfit for human inhabitation and . . . calculated to debase the minds and habits of those whose poverty may drive them to seek shelter in such dens.[20]

Not content with such representations at local level, the residents had written to Chadwick at the General Board of Health in London, as had Mr. Bland himself, offering to attend and explain his plans. At the meeting in Leicester, Stone recorded the unanimous disapproval of the plan unless the number of houses in the yard was reduced from seven to five and a back way provided for rear access. Two days later from the General Board in London there came the evasive reply that 'the Board have no intention of assuming any right as a Court of Appeal in the case of such a complaint', while to the offending builder, it sent what must surely have seemed like an official *carte blanche*, telling him that it could not go into the matter and would not require his attendance.[21] In view of this it is hardly surprising that Bland decided to ignore the Local Board's decision. Indeed, it would appear that he did more than that, for the Ordnance Survey map of 1885 shows not just two, but three mean hovels erected at the far end of the courtyard.

The remarkable fact is not that such houses were allowed, but that a considerable outcry was raised against them on broadly social grounds rather than from motives of self-interest. It was not in fact the first time that the Local Board had crossed swords with Mr. Bland. In March 1852 he had sought permission to erect in Lower Brown Street 13 houses on a similar plan, with nine houses of one room up and one room down, built in a courtyard behind the four houses fronting the street. The plan was amended to allow for only seven houses at the rear and, in this form, was approved by the Board.[22]

On this former occasion, however, no public protest ensued and in the very centre of the town houses were built which were no better than those so passionately opposed on the estate of the Freehold Land Society. It seems clear that initially the Land Society felt responsible for the dwellings erected on its estates. It may be that what was considered deplorable in the newer outskirts of the town could pass unnoticed in its crowded interior, where standards were already much lower. It also seems evident that the surveyors of Leicester were less concerned about standards of house building than were the early officers of health or the Town Clerk, Samuel Stone.

In January 1853, Samuel Stone had called the attention of the General Board of Health to the deficiencies of the Public Health Act in not requiring the builders to state the dimensions of rooms, 'the ventilation etc. and in not giving some express power in these particulars'.[23] When the dispute over Bland's houses arose in August, Stone reminded the General Board of this letter, and observed that the Local Board's powers appeared to be very limited: 'It would, however, be satisfactory to the Local Board to have the opinion of the General Board on the extent of their powers as to the size of and height of rooms—the ventilation—the prevention of back-to-back buildings etc. (against which the Board entertain a strong opinion)'. It would, he said, 'fortify them in any course taken' and serve to guide the General Board in considering the possible extension of the Public Health Act.[24]

Tom Taylor, the Assistant Secretary to the General Board, replied that 'the Board would only suggest that the Local Board be careful in insisting on the provision they make for Water Closets and Drainage in the houses to be built by Mr. Bland'[25] . . . and that the Board agreed with Stone's construction of the Act and his view of what was necessary to improve it, so far as concerned the regulation of building.

This incident illustrates not only the concern of the Local Board and of other influential citizens for housing standards, but also the power of speculative builders under an almost unrestricted system of free enterprise. In the face of this the Board could do little more than tinker with the regulation of such housing. It also confirms once again the limited nature of the controls envisaged by the General Board of

Health: water closets and drainage were its principal concern, not lack of ventilation or the dimensions of rooms, nor even the prevention of back-to-back housing.

Bland was by no means abashed at the public exposure of his cupidity and lack of scruple. A few months later he attended the Board as one of a deputation of proprietors of land in Curzon Street, who sought to maintain private ownership of the road—presumably in order to avoid road charges. The Clerk informed the deputation that the streets were 'dedicated to the public when first opened and that consequently they cannot be reclaimed as private property'.[26]

In 1861, Bland appeared again before the Committee, this time asking permission to put privies into his 17 new houses in Watling Street and to supply them with well water instead of that from the Water Company. He was informed that the usual regulations, obliging builders of new property to connect up with the main drainage and water supply where possible, must be obeyed.[27] Again in 1862 Mr. Bland failed to comply with the bye-laws as to the height of his attics in Lincoln Street; these being 7ft. 10ins. instead of 8ft. high. He promised to be more careful in future.[28]

Bland did not confine his interests to the building of cheap houses, however. His name appeared on the petition of 1856 against any increase in the borough rate[29] and in November 1862 he entered a controversy over the establishment of a Free Library. 'As far as I am concerned', he wrote, 'I object to pay for any man's reading. I can pay for my own, and am not willing to pay for other people's, especially for those that can afford to pay for themselves'.[30]

The following year he was elected as a Liberal on the Council and himself became a member of the Highways and Sewerage Committee. Even then, Bland's effrontery did not cease for he infringed the bye-laws by neglecting to have some of his own property certified.[31]

That such a man could put himself forward as a Liberal candidate alongside such genuine radicals as the Biggses or even Whetstone, suggests that to be a Liberal in Leicester was the only hope for aspiring politicians of the time. It is also a warning against thinking in political stereotypes. By no means all Liberals favoured social reform, for opposition to collectivist policies was the corollary of economic liberalism, and Bland's crude adherence to *laissez-faire* capitalism received wide support in theory, even though it often had to be abandoned in practice.

With the failure of the attempt to stop the erection of Thomas Bland's houses in Curzon Street there seems to have been no further attempt to prevent the erection of cheap housing of the sort which Bland supplied. There were, however, occasional public protests against such confined clusters of cheap houses, and there were unheeded calls for consideration of the environmental needs of the new residential suburbs. Thus when the Danett's Hall estate was sold in 1861 on the death of Dr. Noble, Dr. Barclay regretted that it was not 'secured as a place of recreation for the public—a People's Park'.[32]

The Danett's Hall land was in fact purchased by the Freehold Land Society which set out five new streets, named after the doctor and his daughters—Flora, Clara, Kate, Noble, and Dannett Streets—and laid them out in the customary way with a total of 176 lots ranging from 194½ sq. yds. to 306 sq. yds. in size and with frontages of between 21 and 28 feet. The ample gardens thus provided for were soon, however, crammed in many cases with an intervening row of cottages, with no road frontage, and approached only through passageways built into rows of houses facing on to the street.

Joseph Dare remarked on the King Richard's Road estate in his report for 1872: 'It is discouraging to observe that in several of the newly-built parts of the town, as between Flora Street and Clara Street on King Richard's Road, and other localities, there are inter-buildings springing up between the streets as originally laid out. Rows of scamped tenements approached from the main streets, through narrow arched passages, choke up what ought to be garden and breathing spaces, and completely destroy the comfort and convenience, to say nothing of the health, of the poor possessors . . . The land as at first laid out was not intended to be thus cluttered up by an inferior class of dwellings. I know some who bought or built upon it with this understanding. All this is very bad; and if our bye-laws sanction such crowding of habitations, so much the worse for the bye-laws, which in this respect must be amended, or the town will still be notorious for its unhealthy condition'.[33]

The Freehold Land Society seems to have accepted the fact that there was not sufficient demand for the larger houses and gardens which it had attempted to provide. The very poor just could not afford the higher rents which bigger house plots and gardens entailed.

In its later estates, off Melton Road and in Clarendon Park, the Freehold Land Society laid out plots of narrower frontage and with smaller gardens. By 1897 the Land Society had ceased to function, although its offspring, the Permanent Building Society, was growing steadily. Under the Building Societies Act of 1836 it was illegal for the societies to own land as well as to raise funds for house building. The twin functions of acquiring property for development and of collecting and investing money deposited for the purchase of houses had therefore to be assumed by separate institutions. The Leicester Permanent Building Society thus emerged in order to meet the needs of the Freehold Land Society members.

However, in the 36 years of its existence the Freehold Land Society had made a substantial contribution to the provision of housing in the town. Thirteen estates were laid out in 31 years, divided into upwards of 2,550 allotments.[34] Even if we assume that only one house was erected per allotment, this represents about one-fifth of the additional housing put up in the period 1851–1881. During this time the town had more than doubled its population. That such a phenomenal increase was sustained without any noticeable deterioration in living conditions or density of population is in part a tribute to the vigilance of the Local Council, as Board of Health, and its building inspectors.

From the standpoint of 100 years later, we may well regret that no consideration was given to the environmental planning of Victorian housing estates. What appals us is not so much the lack of bathrooms and water closets, which can be fitted where they are lacking, as the sheer

Fig. 8. Housing in Flora Street, Dannett Street, Clara Street and Noble Street from the O.S. map of 1885

monotony of row after endless row of almost identical houses. It was an aspect of urban living which did not apparently worry the Victorians. They were closer in time and space to the mud and wattle hovels which still served to accommodate many a farm hand, and they exulted in the march of brick and mortar over the countryside. 'From the workmen's tenement', wrote the editor of the *Leicester Chronicle*, 'with its large window panes, and variegated brick front—with its good drainage and gas and water supplies—replacing the old miserable structure of 30 or 40 or more years ago—to the Victorian villa at Stoneygate, in which every convenience and luxury that taste can covet is supplied—there is every graduation of dwelling, evidencing the wonderful advances made of late years in architectural improvement'.[35]

Housing and the Immigrant Irish

But what of the 'submerged tenth', the poor for whom even a modest rent of two shillings and sixpence was too large an outlay from the weekly income? What of those who in fact could not afford accommodation that met the minimum standards allowed by the local authority in new buildings? Such people were inevitably forced into those congested quarters of the town where courts of the meanest design still abounded.

The Irish immigrants, having fled from gruelling poverty in their homeland, were content to settle in such places. Itinerant Irishmen supplemented the local labour force throughout the 19th century, returning to Ireland after helping with the corn harvest. Every summer they would reappear 'with the regularity of swallows',[36] and there were some who settled in England for good. But the famine of 1845–6 turned a trickle into a flood, and like other towns Leicester received its share of these desperate and destitute newcomers. From 477 native-born Irishmen enumerated in the census of 1841 the figure rose to 877 in 1851 or one in 71 of the population. In the immediate years following the famine, immigration was yet more marked and a few particular localities within the town took on the character of Irish enclaves. Abbey Street off Belgrave Gate was one such place. There, according to the census of 1841, one in seven was born in Ireland. Ten years later the proportion was nearly one in four.

These haunts of the Irish became notorious as centres of poverty, sickness and petty crime, often the scene of gang-fighting as racial prejudice fanned the flames of trivial disputes. One such affray in September 1848 appears to have originated in a dispute over sixpence charged by a shoemaker on a Sunday morning. The Irish community felt sufficiently aggrieved to gather about 100 of its compatriots at eight o'clock the same evening and to set upon the English who were driven down Belgrave Gate. A contemporary report tells how at this point 'the English forces became the stronger, for the whole of the Irish were driven back again and had to take refuge in their lodging houses . . . blows were dealt freely and brickbats flying on each side'.[37] When the police were called in they were obliged to 'use the staves very freely upon the insurgents, and to make a large number of prisoners, which with the assistance of the people the police were enabled to do. This was not effected', says the report, 'without several police being bruised, Sergeant Fossit's leg being cut to the bone with a sickle, and Sergeant Tarrat's head being laid open with a brickbat'. The account concludes significantly that out of 37 rioters apprehended only five were resident in the town, all the rest being 'tramps', the residents of lodging houses.

Lodging houses were generally older properties divided into separate rooms for men and women, but the standard of such accommodation varied widely and rooms were often shared by both sexes of all ages. One of the first fruits of sanitary reform in Leicester was the regular inspection of such lodging houses from 1849. The Board of Health recognised minimum standards of cleanliness and specified maximum numbers to inhabit each room. Joseph Dare noted in 1855 that there were 38 such lodging-houses in Leicester, accommodating 587 persons,[38] a figure considerably in excess of that given by Ranald Martin for 1845, when he estimated that 240 people used them nightly.[39] The population had increased by about one-fifth in the intervening years, but the increase in lodging house inmates may well be another reflection of the growth of Irish migrant labour following the potato famine.

One child of Irish immigrants, Tom Barclay, born in 1852 lived to write the story of his life. The Irish, he suggests whimsically, settled in Green Street because they liked the name, and so it became the focal point of their expatriate community. His first home was in a courtyard off Burley's Lane where 'the one door and one chamber window of the two-roomed crib we lived in were seldom opened, though not six feet from the muck hole and the unflushed privies, and air could only get in from one side of the house'.[40] The family moved several times, to a 'similar two-roomed hut' in Abbey Street and then to a 'two-roomed pigsty-crib in a court off Woodboy Street' where his chief memory was of 'alarms and excursions, chases and flights and mad uproar. How could anyone resist breaking out of that dirty kennel on a summer's day?' he asked. When they did venture out the English children greeted them with 'Bad luck to the ship that brought ye over!' and they were 'battered, threatened, elbowed, pressed back to the door of our kennel amid boos and jeers and showers of small missiles'.[41] The English, says Barclay, were regarded with a mixture of contempt and hatred and whenever an Englishman did anything disreputable, his mother was wont to remark: 'Ah well, sure, what better could one expect from the breed of King Harry?'[42]

Every night they would kneel for prayers on the floor where 'bags of dusty rags and putrescent bones were spilled out to be sorted'. Even when nursing her babes his mother had to go to work and Tom had to act as nurse, often putting his tongue into his baby sister's mouth to stop her cries of hunger. 'The cries used to cease for a minute, and then were resumed as the tongue gave no satisfaction. Poor cooped-up vermin-infested brats!' Cleanliness was if anything harder to achieve than godliness. 'I'm sure', he says, 'we never had a complete bath in all our childhood's years . . . Mother did all that was possible, but she had neither time nor means to boil our rags of shirts and sheets when washing'.[43]

Tom Barclay was more interested in people than in houses, but he gives a detailed description of one lodging house, a model one, in Britannia Street. On its front were bas relief figures of the four nationalities, English, Scots, Irish and Welsh, carved out of brickwork. This was the Victoria model lodging house where there were 'enamelled brick lined lavatories and laundries' and lockers to be had for a sixpenny deposit. Framed rules announced the prohibition of alcohol and no smoking upstairs. 'The prices of beds range from 4d. to 8d. The establishment finds all crockery and cooking utensils, but lodgers board themselves,' and says Barclay, 'the cooking ranges would not shame a Stoneygate mansion.'[44]

Barclay's description is much closer to the modern conception of a hostel for vagrants than to the sordid Dickensian dens of his youth, and as the standard of accommodation for migrant labour improved over the years, so too did the housing men came to expect for the resident population. The Board of Health as we have seen did all it could to enforce higher standards upon builders of new houses. But there remained those in the settled population who were unable to afford the rents demanded for such dwellings. To these unfortunates it was no solution to demolish slums. Their basic poverty made them perpetual seekers of the lowest possible class of accommodation. The solution of subsidised housing was not to come until after the First World War, but it was mooted as early as 1888, oddly enough by a Conservative councillor, John Richardson.

The Beginnings of Council Housing in Leicester

Pointing to the 3,000 houses built in courts and squares at the rear of others, Richardson declared that it was no good expecting men who earned 18s. or £1 per week to pay 6s. to 10s. a week for the houses then being erected on the outskirts of the town, and he advocated the building of council flats at 2s. or 2s. 6d. a week.[45] 'As a moderately large rate-payer', said Richardson, he was 'prepared to pay his share towards building and keeping in proper repair the dwellings of artisans', and he believed they were 'legally justified in spending the ratepayers' money for that purpose.'

William Winterton condemned the idea as 'socialistic' and held that the building trade must 'find its own level'. The Council ought not, said Winterton, 'take steps which would end in the destruction of private enterprise'. Thomas Wright, as Mayor, hoped 'nothing of a communistic character' would be done by the Corporation and urged reconsideration of the plan.[46]

Nine years later the Estates Committee again brought up the subject with a proposal to erect blocks of tenement flats in Winifred Street. There were to be 51 such flats built in six groups around a 'miniature oasis' of trees and shrubs. It was proposed to charge 2s. 3d. per week for the single-bedroom flats on the third floor, while those on the second and ground floor paid a little more. The most expensive accommodation was to be in two-bedroomed ground floor flats at 3s. 9d. per week.[47]

Councillor Walters made it clear that 'they wanted to make provision for the very poorest'. The Local Government Board, however, refused to sanction these plans. As a result of its delays and indecision and the revision of plans to meet its requirements, the cost of the scheme rose by £707 above the estimates, necessitating higher rent charges which put the tenements out of reach of the very poor for whom they were intended. 'The experience of the Town Council with reference to the Winifred Street workmen's dwellings is not encouraging to municipal effort', wrote the *Chronicle*, 'One cannot help regretting that the estimates should have to be increased in the way they have for things the local authority did not consider requisite'.[48]

In the event the Winifred Street flats were let at rents varying between 5s. 1½d. for two-bedroomed ground-floor flats, and 3s. for second-floor single tenements. The first block was reported fully occupied by September 1900.[49] The rents are now somewhat higher, but Winifred Street still has its original blocks of Council tenements with a 'miniature oasis' of trees between them.

The beginnings of council housing in Leicester are not to be compared with the imaginative and visionary achievements of Saltaire or Bournville, but they stand comparison with municipal housing in towns like Liverpool and Glasgow, where the gaunt blocks of working-class flats erected early in the 20th century have now become ugly slums as depressing and more permanent than the private enterprise hovels they once replaced. One great advantage of the Leicester scheme was its relatively small scale. Two blocks of flats cannot so readily degenerate as can 10 or 20 identical blocks, and the improvements on which the Local Government Board insisted have doubtless rendered them more acceptable to later generations.

Chapter Seven

WATERING THE TOWN

ADEQUATE PROVISION of fresh water was a cardinal precept of sanitarian reformers and as we have seen, the Leicester Waterworks Company had close links with the Town Council from its inception. Had it not been for the support of the Council the town would have waited much longer for proper supplies, and it was only the guarantee of four per cent. profit to shareholders for 30 years that induced private investors to part with their money.

Despite the early misgivings of investors and ratepayers, the Waterworks Company, supported by the Corporation guarantee, proved a complete success. Appropriately the first building to receive its supplies from the new reservoir at Thornton was the Temperance Hall on 21 December 1853.[1]

Thornton continued to supply 1,600,000 gallons per day for the next 13 years, but by the mid 1860s its capacity was becoming insufficient as the town expanded, and the Local Board of Health obliged builders to connect new houses to the Company's water instead of sinking wells.

By December 1864 dwindling supplies at Thornton led to appeals to the public not to waste water.[2] Hawkesley blamed defective water closets for much of the wastage, but the main cause of the water shortage was a run of exceptionally dry summers. The directors recognised that while such circumstances might explain the heavy demands on Thornton reservoir such problems were likely to recur, and the Company had to make provision for a large increase in its storage capacity.

In June 1865, therefore, it applied to parliament for powers to extend its works, and in September Hawkesley reported on a number of possible locations for new reservoirs, coming down firmly in favour of tapping the Lin brook at Bradgate: 'The finest stream, the best water, the cleanest drainage, and under all conditions except that of pumping the most advantageous scheme is the Bradgate'.[3] Six weeks later he remarked that, 'if the town of Leicester obtains possession of this very advantageous source no (other) town in the kingdom will be better supplied with water for many years to come'.[4]

The Bill to enable the Company to construct the Bradgate or Cropston reservoir encountered some opposition from the Council. The Company sought to obtain powers to limit its supplies in emergency to an intermittent flow instead of constant supply, but the Council objected to the inconvenience and annoyance that would result from such a provision. The Council also sought permission to use portable instead of fixed meters at its hydrants as an economy measure. Both these points were conceded and the Bill passed in May 1866, the Corporation taking a share in the new capital.[5] One hundred and eighty acres of land had already been purchased from the Earl of Stamford, and the new reservoir was completed in 1870.

Cropston added 500 million gallons to the supply from Thornton, yet so rapidly was the demand increasing that Hawkesley immediately began to give warning of the need to conserve supplies. In 1874 the Company decided to extend the Cropston works and therefore sought new borrowing powers. At the same time it was suggested that the Council might at this juncture forgo its right to a half share in the profits of any such additional investment by the Company.[6] The Council's original stake in the undertaking had paid handsome dividends, and as the shareholders were now only too anxious to subscribe more capital, the Company's request seemed a reasonable one. It was, however, the beginning of a process which was to lead to the extinction of the private Company altogether.

By a curious irony, it was a prominent Conservative who publicly mooted the idea of municipal ownership in Leicester—William Winterton, who had become Chairman of the Highways and Sewerage Committee in 1873.[7]

Winterton, 'a stiff Presbyterian of the Scottish Kirk',[8] never minced his words, bullied his way through committee meetings and frequently lost his temper with his supporters as well as his opponents. It is hard to imagine how he would have survived in an age of rigid party discipline. In 1876 he became first Mayor to the reformed Corporation to be chosen from outside the Liberal ranks. Proposing him, Alderman Stevenson remarked that 'his views were generally of so enlightened and liberal a nature that it was only on very rare occasions that the most advanced Radical would find it necessary to dissent from them'.[9]

In November 1874 Winterton declared his belief that the time had arrived when the Corporation should negotiate for the outright purchase of the Waterworks Company, and he made a formal proposition to this effect. Battle was joined. The Waterworks Company applied for sanction to raise further share capital and proposed the end of the arrangement whereby the Council took 50 per cent. of the surplus profits.[10]

Winterton's case rested on the need to facilitate the closure of wells in the town centre, and to vest the supply of water with the same authority as that which had responsibility for public health. At the time 7,000 houses were supplied with pump water, while increasing overcrowding in the centre meant that this water was often 'contaminated by the refuse from the drains'.[11] Municipal ownership might also facilitate the substitution of water closets for more primitive means of sewage disposal. The Local Board had disallowed cesspools since December 1857, where it was possible to connect the drains to the main sewer network, but there was evidently some reluctance on the part of the Waterworks Company to extend its supply just for water closets. The effect, as John Moore pointed out in his report of 1856, was to limit conversion to water closets and to prolong the use of open privies and cesspools. He urged the Company to rescind its policy, but the plea fell on deaf ears, for 10 years later he reiterated his concern, claiming that 'privy cesspools' would be 'to a great extent abolished, but for the stringent regulations of the Water Works Company, who refuse to supply water for water closets unless it is also taken for household purposes'.[12]

To the sanitarian arguments for municipal ownership, Winterton added an economic one. If the works were to be purchased at all, it would be better to buy soon than wait until dividends and the value of the works rose further.

The battle lines were indeed oddly drawn, with the leading Conservative urging his Liberal adversaries not to continue in the old groove, and the Tory press praising the 'new Groove' as 'wider, safer and more beneficial' than that in which the town had been 'sliding for the last thirty years'.[13] James Thompson, implacably opposed to the scheme, saw in this enthusiasm a sinister plot to bring the Tories to power 'with the help of Radical allies, under the pretext of the waterworks purchase',[14] a suggestion that tacitly admits the popularity of the scheme.

The allegation of a Radical-Conservative alliance recalls the Improvement Debate a generation earlier, when the *Leicester Journal* relinquished its customary adherence to economy and came out strongly in support of William Biggs and the improvers: 'The ratepayers must not allow themselves to be misled in these matters:—their true interests lie in progressive improvements. When a town rises to importance, its public buildings—its widened streets—its comforts, and its means of paying for them, generally keep pace with its prosperity . . . Thus may it be with Leicester'.[15] In 1846 the *Journal* urged its readers to support the purchase of the private waterworks company on the Chadwickian premises that money spent on public improvement would eventually lead to lower expenditure in poor rates: 'True economy is not always best promoted by drawing tight your purse strings; a liberal and judicious outlay will often prevent great and irretrievable losses. If attention had been paid to the sanitary condition of Leicester for the last twenty years, an immense amount of money loss might have been saved to the inhabitants, independently of the diminution of sickness and pain, and premature deaths . . . what will have to be paid in Borough Rates may be saved out of the Poor Rates and the profits arising from increased prosperity'.[16]

In 1849 it was, however, legally impossible for the Corporation to undertake the construction of the Thornton works because of the clause in the Public Health Act which gave preference to private companies. It was therefore unjust of Winterton to rebuke the Council in 1877 for its 'feeble action' in not having purchased the works when they were first originated.[17]

The case for municipalisation received a sharp setback early in 1875, when the Company's lawyer revealed that the clause enabling the Council to purchase the works in the Bill of 1851 had lapsed, and that no such provision had been incorporated in the Act of 1866.[18] Even E. S. Ellis was evidently ignorant of this important omission until January 1875, and it was an unfortunate reflection on the competence of two men whose sagacity and wisdom in the affairs of the borough had become almost legendary, Samuel Stone, the former Clerk, and Joseph Whetstone, the erstwhile Chairman of the Highways and Sewerage Committee. If the Council wished to purchase the works, it could legally enforce its claim only upon the original establishment at Thornton.

This news did not, as the *Leicester Chronicle* suggested, bring about 'the sudden and complete collapse of the case for the Corporation',[19] but it did mean a protracted legal battle in which the Council invoked powers of compulsory purchase when the Company declined to state a price for their undertaking. Winterton's advocacy of municipal control led him to question the whole concept of financial orthodoxy upon which Whetstone and the economists had based their policy. Debt, he pointed out, was a relative matter. 'What was a heavy debt?' he asked, 'A man of small means, who could brag that he owed very little, might be poor nonetheless; but a man might owe immense sums, and yet be immensely rich . . . A debt of £400,000 was a mere nothing, if they possessed property that was as fully an equivalent; indeed the advantages that were to be gained in a sanitary point of view fully balanced such an outlay'. He asked the more cautious citizens to remember that 'during the previous year alone the rateable value had increased to something like £11,000'.[20]

Beyond the financial argument, however, was the need to provide an adequate supply of drinking water. Winterton took the view that public ownership was necessary in order to carry out the policy of the Highways and Sewerage Committee with regard to the closure of wells. Seven thousand houses continued to rely on drinking water pumped from wells within the borough, while increasing overcrowding meant that water was often 'contaminated by the refuse from the drains'.[21] Such contamination was apparently in part the result of deliberate policy. A witness to Ranger's enquiry in 1849 had stated that soil pits were dug deep in order that they might drain into the water table and so avoid the expense of periodic emptying. The 'principal well-digger' of the town stated that for over 30 years he had followed this practice, and numerous instances were given of water being infected from the soil pits.[22]

In Winterton's view, the Council 'had no right to part with the lives and health of Leicester for a mere question of income; but ought to value persons' lives more highly'.[23] As 'one of the first necessaries of life', water, said Winterton, should be in the hands of those members of the municipal committees who had the care and management and were responsible for the good health, comfort and decency of the population.[24]

Feelings ran high over the issue of purchase and both sides indulged in a certain amount of recrimination, especially after the failure of the Corporation's attempts to purchase the Waterworks Company in March 1875. Alderman Burgess, a brother-in-law of E. S. Ellis, claimed that there had been 'a persistent effort . . . to depreciate the value of the shares', in order to make their purchase more attractive to the ratepayers. 'This was enough', said Burgess, 'to set any directors against any friendly negotiations'.[25] It was also alleged that the pro-purchase party engineered the election of the new Mayor, Alderman Barfoot, in order to promote their own cause.[26] Barfoot cut a poor figure as chief magistrate, and when cross-questioned at Westminster during the committee stage of the Corporation's Bill to purchase the Waterworks Company, he confessed his ignorance of the terms of the Public Health Act of 1875. This, according to the Company's counsel, would have given the Corporation all the powers they needed to oblige house owners to lay on piped water instead of using wells. The *Leicester Chronicle* inveighed against the 'pitiable exhibition' which the Mayor made of himself in front of the Committee: 'A more thorough and discreditable failure has, we fancy, never engaged the attention of a House of Commons Committee or disgraced a Mayor and Corporation within the memory of man, than that of the attempt of our Leicester Town Council to procure the power to purchase the Waterworks. It really is painful and humiliating'.[27]

According to Winterton, however, the Sanitary Committee was well aware of the terms of the Public Health Act; the town clerk had already been in correspondence with the Local Government Board and his recommendations incorporated into the Waterworks Bill.[28]

Two years later passions had cooled, and the Waterworks Company itself made a free offer of sale to the Corporation in return for interest at one per cent. above the current rate earned on its shares. Winterton, still in the Mayoral seat, seized the offer with alacrity. Negotiations began almost immediately and the works were finally transferred to the Corporation on 2 September 1878.[29]

Buying the Gas Works

By contrast with the bitter and protracted debate over municipal ownership of the water supply, the purchase of the Gas Company was carried through with astonishing speed and unanimity. Formed in 1821 with a share capital of £24,000 and 24 shareholders, the Gas Company had steadily grown with the increasing demands of domestic, municipal and industrial users, while the price of gas fell gradually from 12 shillings per 100 cubic feet to 2s. 10d. in 1877.[30] This apparent altruism on the part of the directors arose from a clause in the Company's charter whereby it had to give the community the benefit of any profits above a dividend of eight per cent. The gasworks apparently made so much money that according to Alderman Grimsley 'the shareholders did not know what to do with it . . . they could not possibly divide it, because the law prohibited that'.[31]

The directors of the gas company proposed to obviate this legal restriction by the issue of additional stock to their shareholders. Before they could do this, however, a Mr. Raikes gave notice in the House of Commons that he intended to introduce in all future Bills relating to gas undertakings a clause compelling directors to issue only fully paid-up shares and to submit them by auction or tender to the highest bidder.[32] Deprived thus of any opportunity of benefiting from their monopoly position, the directors approached Grimsley, the Chairman of the Highways and Sewerage Committee, and Winterton, with a view to selling the works to the Corporation without the expense of a Parliamentary Bill. Agreement was reached on terms in April 1877 and parliamentary sanction to purchase was included with that for buying the Waterworks, the Bill receiving Royal Assent on 4 July 1878.[33]

Burdening the Borough

The purchase of the gas and water companies ushered in a new era of municipal finance. In 1836 the borough debt had been viewed with righteous indignation by the Liberals as a scandalous legacy of their profligate Tory predecessors. The debts of the old Corporation amounted to £30,564 and in addition there was £7,250 owed by Thomas Burbidge, the former Town Clerk, to Sir Thomas White's charity which the Court of Chancery required the Council to pay.[34] No wonder Samuel Stone jibbed at the thought of paying Burbidge compensation for loss of his office.

In its first 10 years the new Corporation managed to keep expenditure down to about £30,000 a year, a modest total for a town of over 48,000 people at the census of 1841. Most of its expenditure was on the setting up of the new police force, to which the exchequer contributed half, and on the upkeep of main streets and markets and the payment of those Corporation officials whose functions were deemed still worthy of support by the re-formed Council.

TOTAL BOROUGH DEBT for the Years 1854 to 1914

	£		£
1854	82,797	1885	1,538,487
1855	88,199	1886	1,639,869
1856	90,749	1887	1,680,792
1857	89,599	1888	1,717,275
1858	88,749	1889	1,765,369
1859	96,551	1890	1,816,475
1860	100,299	1891	1,902,003
1861	96,849	1892	2,091,830
1862	95,050	1893	2,201,468
1863	missing	1894	2,230,855
1864	92,015	1895	2,398,313
1865	87,365	1896	2,450,730
1866	95,880	1897	2,553,109
1867	missing	1898	2,688,213
1868	128,589	1899	2,921,053
1869	144,147	1900	3,259,579
1870	163,442	1901	3,295,698
1871	169,567	1902	3,677,462
1872	190,692	1903	3,757,995
1873	199,949	1904	4,432,897
1874	211,433	1905	5,163,221
1875	221,898	1906	5,201,224
1876	247,764	1907	5,152,125
1877	269,963	1908	5,074,685
1878	286,525	1909	5,045,554
1879	985,604	1910	5,060,476
1880	1,397,428	1911	5,005,817
1881	1,479,076	1912	4,901,117
1882	1,508,652	1913	4,865,336
1883	1,514,782	1914	4,754,284
1884	1,514,931		

With the establishment of the Board of Health, the Council's expenses began to mount steadily and there was a corresponding leap in the rates, from an average of ninepence in the years 1845 to 1849 to 2s. 3d. in 1850.[35] The steep rise in rates reflects Whetstone's belief that capital sums borrowed on the security of the rates ought to be repaid as soon as possible.

In the quarter century after 1851 about a third of the total expenditure of the Corporation was for outlay connected with the Board of Health, such as scavenging, street lighting and the construction of the sewerage system; though, in the mid '50s, the proportion rose to very nearly half while the initial costs of the sewerage scheme were at their highest.

The level of municipal rates remained below three shillings until 1869, climbed to 4s. 6d. in 1876, and fluctuated between 3s. 6d. and 5s. 0d. till the end of the century. It is true, as Winterton pointed out, that the expansion of the town brought a higher rateable value of property, but this was far from equal to the rise in civic expenditure and it was only by adding to its long-term debts that the relative stability of the borough rates was maintained. Thus the municipal debt increased dramatically with the acquisition of the gas and water undertakings in the late 1870s, rising from a total of under £300,000 in 1878 to £1,500,000 in 1882. Thereafter the cost of sewerage and flood works contributed to a steady rise over the next decade to £2 million in 1892; while additional expenditure on gas and water undertakings led the total debt to rise by a further million by the end of the century.

No other department of the Corporation contributed so much to the mounting total of municipal liabilities as the gas and water departments. By 1913 when the total debt stood at £4,865,336, the capital expended on the gas and water undertakings amounted to £2,640,668. Yet despite this heavy capital outlay, both departments returned a handsome profit to the Corporation.

Fears of municipal incompetence in the management of the concerns proved quite groundless. The *Leicester Chronicle*, which had so often predicted disaster, admitted in 1881 that: 'the financial benefits derived by the borough through the acquisition of these great undertakings was becoming more and more apparent'.[36] Noting the substantial profits of each department, the *Chronicle* observed that these enabled the borough to finance great improvements in the town and to offset the demands of the School Board upon the rates; an observation which led a correspondent to complain of an unjust tax on the consumer since gas prices could have been further reduced if the excess profits had not been put to relief of the rates.[37]

The Search for New Water Supplies

Municipal purchase had little effect on the actual operation of the waterworks, its personnel and policies remaining unaffected by the change in ownership. Thomas Hawkesley, who had been Engineer to the Company since its inception, continued to give warning of the need for fresh supplies.[38] In 1885 he counselled the acquisition of the old canal reservoir at Blackbrook to the north of Charnwood Forest, dismissing a number of alternative suggestions including the Saddington and Naseby reservoirs.[39] Hawkesley was probably the foremost water engineer of his day, having by this time constructed over 120 reservoirs.

While the Corporation deliberated over this proposal, Loughborough, 10 miles north of Leicester and geographically much closer to Blackbrook reservoir, awakened to its own needs. Hawkesley admitted that Blackbrook 'naturally' belonged to Loughborough rather than Leicester; and the Town Council of Loughborough, acting with uncommon energy, negotiated with Mr. de Lisle, the owner of Garendon, through which the brook runs, for the purchase of two fields abutting on the brook, and thereby acquired riparian rights.[40]

Both Loughborough and Leicester therefore presented Bills to parliament in 1885 for the acquisition of the same water supply. A poll of the town in Leicester found two-thirds in favour of the scheme, but parliament came down firmly in favour of Loughborough's claim. The Water Committee at Leicester was reduced to the expedient of raising the sill of Cropston reservoir by two feet in 1887 and that of Thornton by one foot two years later.[41]

In November 1886 Hawkesley reported on possible alternative supplies from the Lingdale, Swithland and Hallgate brooks, but the idea met with little enthusiasm until 1889, when negotiations for Swithland began in earnest.[42] There was formidable opposition, however, from Lord Lanesborough.

Even after May 1890 when the Leicester Waterworks Act received Royal Assent, there was a legal battle over the compensation to which the Earl was entitled. His Lordship claimed £61,312 for 225 acres of land exclusive of timber, while the Corporation's arbitrator proposed £18,700. Fortunately for Leicester, the umpire fixed on a sum of £27,800 including the value of timber.[43]

Swithland reservoir was the first major waterworks in which J. B. Everard was engaged. Everard had long been an architect and engineer of repute in Leicester, having designed, among other things, the cattle market in 1872 and the Corporation baths of 1879. As Thomas Hawkesley's long and distinguished career neared its end, Everard slipped into his place as chief adviser to the water company.[44] Thus it was, in 1898, that Everard was asked to report on yet further possible sources of water.

Everard realised that any additional supply from Leicestershire itself would merely offer a palliative, and that the ultimate source of fresh supplies had to be much further afield. His prophetic insight and imagination led him to devise what came to be known as the Derwent Valley Scheme. Once again, Leicester met resistance from rival claimants. Derby and Nottingham regarded the Derwent as their natural supply, but with diplomacy and determination an amicable solution was agreed whereby the waters of the Derwent were divided between the three towns. The scheme received Royal Assent on 1 August 1899 and was completed in 1912.[45]

Testing the Waters

Throughout its history the Waterworks Company had endeavoured to maintain the highest standards of purity in its supplies. Indeed the chief argument for constructing the works as well as for municipal ownership was the need to close down polluted wells and substitute a wholesome supply of drinking water. But what was pure drinking water? In the context of contemporary medical and scientific knowledge, it was only possible to offer the crudest definition of purity. When

John Moore reported on the water supply of two yards in Braunstone Gate in 1854, he found it 'so bad in smell and taste as to be unfit for use as a beverage or culinary purposes'.[46]

It will be remembered that this was the same year in which Dr. John Snow published his famous findings on the water-borne nature of cholera, and it was not until 20 years later that the work of Koch and Pasteur entered into the accepted canons of scientific orthodoxy. By 1867 Wyatt Crane reported that it was 'well understood that both Typhoid Fever and cholera are propagated as much from impure water, contaminated by foecal matter, and containing the germs of these diseases, as from aerial emanations from these agents'.[47]

By 1873, the sanitary inspectors were being asked to report on the purity of water as well as on the adequacy of supply, but the problem of definition remained. Chemical tests on various samples of well, river and sewage waters were carried out by Professors Aikin and Taylor of Guy's Hospital before the establishment of the works at Thornton in 1851, and according to George Bown even earlier tests of this sort were made on samples of water in the town.[48]

Regular tests on the chemical content of various water supplies were carried out on the appointment of William Young as Public Analyst in 1872; his appointment being a joint one to the borough and county sanitary authorities. But chemical tests were not always valid, as the champions of the new science of bacteriology began to point out. The absence of any agreed criteria by which the content of water could be judged posed a problem for the sanitary authorities. By what standards should water be judged? And on what grounds should wells be closed? The Leicester Sanitary Committee found a solution in its own deductions as to what constituted purity in the local context.

The issue was spelled out with admirable clarity in the report of the Medical Officer of Health for 1881: 'However desirable it would be for health authorities to have a fixed standard of purity for universal application in the analyses of well waters throughout the country, it is simply impossible to construct such a standard for the variations of subsoil everywhere met with and manifold sources from which organic principles in surface waters are derived. The best method of obtaining a standard of purity . . . is to ascertain by frequent borings the character and proportions of the constituents, therefore the natural water of the district. When tested by such a measure, the analysis of well water, if polluted only to a slight extent, will always give results amounting to positive proof of pollution having taken place, and thus, while no injustice is done to owners of house property, the health of the consumers is safely guarded'.[49]

It is unlikely that any more scientific approach could have been adopted at this time. Many local authorities were much slower to awaken to the need for objective chemical analysis of their water supplies. The standards of the Urban District Council of Hinckley in south-west Leicestershire were evidently lower than those of the county town, for in 1891, Hinckley began to take water from Snareston colliery, the water from which had been rejected by Leicester when 'an analysis of the liquid procurable at Snareston proved it to be unsuitable'.[50]

Gradual enforcement of greater stringency in testing, and a policy of anticipating complaint rather than waiting for the public to request the analysis of well waters, led to the virtual elimination of wells for drinking purposes within the borough. New tests devised by the medical officer in 1881 ascertained chloride content, smell when heated to 100 deg. F., nitrogen as nitrates, ammonia content, albumenoid ammonia, and total solids at 42 deg. F. By this test 78.8 per cent. of the samples tested were condemned, or 56 out of 71 wells analysed, instead of the 42.7 per cent. in the previous six-year period.[51] In 1883 85 per cent. of the samples were condemned, and in 1884, 70 per cent.[52]

The posts of Medical Officer and Public Analyst were combined in the following year and the first municipal laboratory in Leicester was established. There were by that time 469 wells supplying 978 houses compared with the 2,800 wells that existed in 1849, and by 1886 the number had fallen to three hundred and sixty. The progressive substitution of piped water for these wells was not simply the result of official condemnation, for well water tended to be excessively hard and unpalatable, so that the handful of wells remaining at the close of the century were confined to industrial use and no longer constituted part of the town's supply of drinking water.[53]

Fig. 9. 'Elmfield', from the drawing by Anne Gregson

Chapter Eight

GREATER LEICESTER

IT IS PERHAPS SIGNIFICANT that Joseph Whetstone had died before the final decision was taken to replace the town hall. His counsel was invariably against spending money on what he regarded as luxury. But by the 1860s the administration of town government was scattered in a growing number of different buildings throughout the centre of the town, and the inconvenience of this, as well as the lack of comfort in the guildhall, necessitated some new arrangement. The judges had for some time refused to sit there, and in December 1870 it was decided at last to put up a new building.[1]

The decision to erect new municipal offices was followed by a protracted dispute over the choice of a suitable site. Two places were canvassed and both had their ardent advocates. One site was in Horsefair Street, where the old cattle market was scheduled for removal under an Improvement Act of 1866. By 1868, however, considerable opposition had mounted to the proposed removal. Traders and publicans joined with farmers in an outcry against the enforced move to Welford Road.[2] Advocates of the cattle market site were suspected of attempting to override opponents of the move by condemning the alternative site.[3] This alternative was a piece of land in Friar Lane. The site had the advantage of being immediately available and it afforded opportunity for centrally-placed offices with frontage on two main streets, yet it was small enough to preclude any extravagant use of public funds. The drawback to the site was that it lay directly on the line of two existing streets which it would be desirable to link together, an operation which would severely restrict the remaining building space

When Samuel Stone pointed out that whatever the Council decided with regard to the town hall, they were bound to proceed with a new cattle market on Welford Road, there were some who doubted his opinion and felt that the town was being forced into vast and unnecessary expense because of a legal technicality.[4] A barrister-at-law pronounced the Act of 1866 to be authoritative only and not compulsory, saying that money was 'not likely' to have been set aside specifically to finance the removal.[5] Stone was outraged at this. Doubtless the slight on his competence touched him almost as much as the insult to his veracity. He declared that he cared more for his character than for 20 cattle markets and pointed out that the Council had in fact borrowed £5,000 for the especial purpose of making the new market.[6] Further legal opinion served only to confirm Stone's view, and the town was obliged to erect a new cattle market and to remove the old one from the town centre.[7] The issue of the site for new municipal buildings was thus decided by default.

It was symptomatic of the Council's ambivalence towards such expenditure that the new building did not include a large room for public assemblies. This was felt to be unnecessary in view of the existence of the Temperance Hall. Nevertheless, force of habit and an irresistible temptation to abbreviate led people to refer to the new offices as the 'Town Hall', and the misnomer was given official recognition in a resolution of the Council in March 1876 which designated the buildings then nearing completion as the 'Town Hall of the Borough of Leicester'.[8]

The new town hall was built at a total cost of £52,911. Its style came in for considerable criticism from contemporaries. It was too austere for lovers of decorative Gothic and for this we must be grateful. Hames's design has a dignity and modest grandeur that marks it as one of the best municipal edifices of its age. Israel Hart, with that mixture of benevolence and panache which eventually won him a knighthood, donated a fine ornamental fountain to adorn the untidy space in front of the new offices.[9] The technical difficulties in supplying a gushing fount of water led Hames to concentrate on the grandeur of the bronze lions in his design rather than on the intermittent dribble emitted from the saucer on their heads.

Thus ended the controversy that had excited so much passion and divided the Liberal establishment since the 1840s. Joseph Whetstone was no longer there able to plead the greater claim of drains and sewers on the civic purse.[10] John Biggs would have rejoiced at the realisation of his long-cherished dream, despite its failure to cater for oratorical talents in an assembly hall; but Biggs, too, was dead.[11] His brother William lived on till 1881, but he lived in Manchester and had long since resigned the civic battles of his native town to other men.[12] In the 1870s, however, it was the financial philosophy of the Biggs brothers that was in the ascendant. Whetstone's concern for economy and frugality in municipal affairs was suddenly forgotten. In its place was a bold acceptance of municipal indebtedness, and a realisation that as the town itself increased so also must the cost of its government. But there was also a realisation that indebtedness was not a thing to be ashamed of. The town was not an individual having to keep within his current means, but a corporate body ministering to the needs of future generations as well as to the present, and as much of its expenditure on civic improvements like the town hall would benefit future citizens, there was good reason to expect posterity to pay some of the bill. Henceforth, the cost of work undertaken by the Corporation would be met by heavy and permanent municipal debt, with the interest on such loans secured out of the rates. Thus while the borough debt stood at £247,764 in 1876, the figure grew tenfold by 1896 and doubled again to £5,202,224 in 1906.

The financial purism which led to Whetstone's constant endeavour to reduce the town's debt, and thereby the burden on future ratepayers, was gradually being discarded. In its place was a civic gospel not unlike that of John and William Biggs, resting not only upon the knowledge that municipal income had increased, but also on the belief that future generations should be expected to pay for the benefits accorded them by their forebears. The financial rationale of municipal socialism was becoming acceptable.

The Retirement of Samuel Stone

The new men who guided the fortunes of Leicester from the 1870s lacked the inestimable advantage of the services of Samuel Stone, the Town Clerk since the birth of the reformed Corporation. Stone suffered increasing infirmity during his last years and felt obliged to resign in September 1872. His grasp of municipal affairs was probably unsurpassed in England at the time. His advice was frequently sought by other localities in the drawing up and execution of bye-laws.[13] His perspicacious remarks on any new legislation were always tendered to the Council with a deference and detachment which disguised the influence that his own opinion had upon the deliberations of elected councillors. He was, as the Rev. C. C. Coe, the minister at the Great Meeting, said of him, 'essentially a moderate man holding his own convictions faithfully and conscientiously and defending them vigorously if need be, but never in the spirit of blind or angry partizanship'. To write his life in full, said Coe, 'would be to reproduce the history of Leicester for the last 40 years . . . He served this town as towns are seldom served; he organised the institutions in the midst of which we live; he advised the magistrates upon the bench, and the councillor in the council chamber and in the committee room'.[14]

The silence of James Thompson on Stone's death in February 1874 is as unaccountable today as it was to some contemporaries. But if his work was not always appreciated in his lifetime, his loss was increasingly apparent thereafter. 'His great and intimate knowledge of local affairs, his remembrance of matters which others had forgotten, his acquaintance with the ramifications of various important subjects—all rendered his loss one that it would be difficult equally to over-estimate and for which to provide a compensating equivalent', wrote Thompson some months later.[15]

Stone's successor was a respected local solicitor, George Toller, whose appointment gave immediate satisfaction on all sides. He was a popular figure who had twice been chosen as Mayor, in 1851 and 1862, and there was every reason to think that he would make an excellent choice as Clerk. The clerkship had rested so easily on his predecessor, however, that Toller failed to appreciate its full burden. Six weeks after taking office he tendered his resignation, admitting that he had not 'sufficiently appreciated the strain involved in the pressure of its multifarious duties'.[16]

The choice of a successor now fell on Thomas Standbridge, the son of a town clerk of Birmingham. He came with glowing references and enjoyed the sympathetic goodwill of the entire Council on his appointment in December 1872. Within a few months his limitations became apparent. He was lazy and incompetent and within a year of his appointment the Mayor, Alderman Stafford, asked him to resign.[17]

In April 1873, when acquainted with Alderman Stafford's views, Standbridge 'cried most bitterly' and there were fears that he might injure himself. Standbridge's father-in-law, summoned from Birmingham, told a number of senior aldermen that 'Tom's father was Town Clerk of Birmingham for many years but was an idle man, and Tom seems to have his father's idleness but not his ability'.[18] An embarrassing episode followed in which Standbridge attempted to answer his critics and refused to resign. In the end the Council was forced to take decisive action and agreed to Winterton's motion that he should immediately cease to hold office.[19]

While the inadequacies of his successors made the Council ever more conscious of the ability of Samuel Stone, it was also increasingly aware of the debt it owed to his chief clerk, John Storey. On the resignation of Toller, the mayor remarked that he did not know what they would have done without the services of Storey, especially during the conduct of the November elections. Storey had been trained to deal with all the routine work of Stone's office and his abilities met with universal approbation, but he lacked any legal qualifications. This in the opinion of the Corporation rendered it impossible to appoint him as Town Clerk.

However, as the shortcomings of Standbridge became more and more obvious, the Council veered to the view that professional qualifications were of less worth than practical competence. On the departure of Standbridge, Storey was appointed Town Clerk, 'during pleasure, at the salary of £160 per annum' as a temporary arrangement.[20] Alderman Foxton declared that Storey was 'well qualified to discharge the duties of the office, and possessed considerable ability, great zeal, and unflinching integrity and industry'.[21]

It was doubtless an additional recommendation that the Council now had an able and efficient town clerk at less than a quarter the salary it paid to his predecessor. A year later the temporary appointment was extended and Storey's salary was raised to £300 per annum. The mayor testified to his legal skill, recalling that he had recently been in the town clerk's office 'when two telegrams arrived from eminent solicitors asking Storey's advice upon points connected with the School Board elections'.[22] Winterton interjected that, 'if Mr. Storey had sat in some of the law courts, and had eaten a number of good dinners, they would have been told that he was competent'.[23] On Storey's appointment as Town Clerk it was arranged that Richard Toller, nephew of the Clerk to the Peace of the same name, should act as Town Solicitor, to deal with matters requiring specific legal expertise beyond the skill of the town clerk. Toller occupied this position for 10 years after which the office was merged again with the Clerkship, Storey having become a qualified solicitor some time before this.

When Storey retired in 1894 to go into private practice, the plaudits of the Council were as unanimous and fulsome as they had been throughout his period of office. An outsider's confirmation of this high testimony came from Major Tulloch, Chief Inspector of the Local Government Board, who wrote to the mayor, saying that he has always openly expressed his admiration of the manner in which the business of Leicester had been conducted: 'Indeed I personally, do not know of any town in the Kingdom where the work has been done better'.[24]

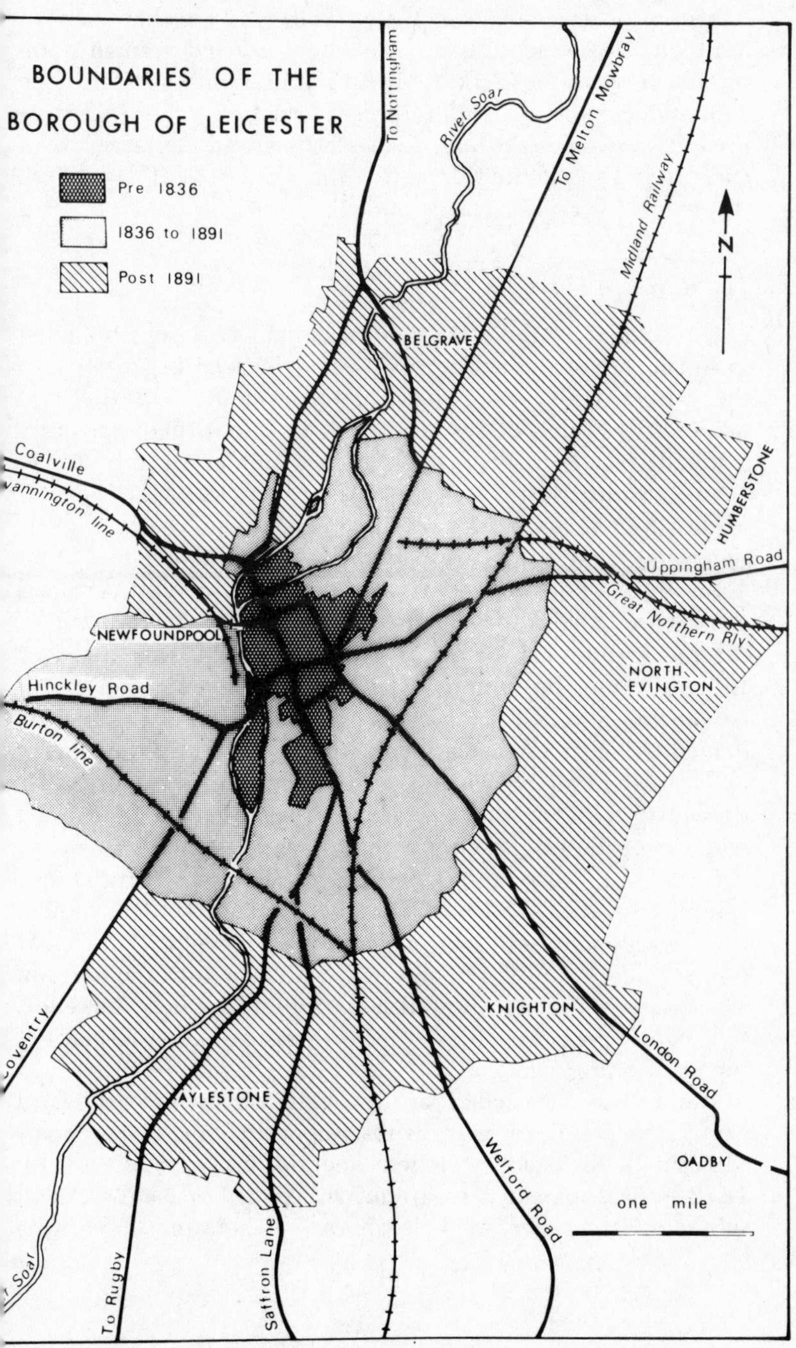

. 10. Boundaries of the Borough of Leicester

Storey's successor was James Bell, yet another man of more than average ability, who later received a knighthood for his services as Clerk to the City of London.[25] With the lamentable exception therefore of the two years following the resignation of Stone, Leicester enjoyed the services of exceptionally talented men in the office of Town Clerk throughout the Victorian period.

The Borough Surveyor

Unfortunately the same cannot be said of those who acted as Borough Surveyor. The post was of crucial importance to the whole concept of town improvement, and the vast scope of official duties attached to the office was only gradually realised even by the first holder of the office. Samuel Smith Harris accepted the post in 1849 for the sum of £150, a salary which even at that time was not over-generous, though higher than the £100 that had to satisfy John Buck, the Medical Officer. Harris probably accepted the office partly for altruistic reasons, for he had earlier offered to draw up a plan of the town at his own expense.[26] In any event he found it galling to have accusations of corruption levelled at him in 1855.[27] Harris indignantly denied the charges, demanded a full enquiry into the matter, and called for a review of his remuneration and duties. He drew up a list of the jobs he was expected to do, ending with the following summary of his various duties, namely: 'to set out work and superintend all the street labour, trapping grates etc.; keep account of men's time; pay them their wages and kept out of money a fortnight. Work eight hours a day for nothing, and called a rogue into the bargain. These are some of the duties of the Borough Surveyor. Who does not envy him?'[28] One suspects he was glad of the excuse to resign.

Harris was succeeded as Borough Surveyor by Edward Loney Stephens, a man whose appetite for work seems sometimes to have stretched beyond his capabilities. By 1872 he was expected to attend an average of eight Council sub-committees per week, each of which lasted about two hours, and to discharge a growing number of routine duties in the oversight of roads, sewers and public works, as well as the inspection of all new buildings, and alterations of existing buildings, three times in the course of construction. At the same time he undertook work in a private capacity as an architect and surveyor, obtaining the consent of the Corporation where major projects were concerned, as in 1857 when he designed a sewerage system for Melton Mowbray.[29] In 1872 a minor storm broke over the failure of the drainage system at the town gaol. Stephens explained that 'an immense dishcloth' had stopped the drain, and the removal of this was complicated by the absence of any plan of drainage for the building.

It was not an isolated incident and Stephen's ability to undertake satisfactorily all his varied duties was openly called in question. Alderman Burgess, while exonerating Stephens from any imputation of indolence stated that 'he undertook to do too much, and could not do it'.[30] The Conservative Chairman of the Highways and Sewerage Committee remarked that when the committee considered the Surveyor's duties, they thought it would be more economical to get one man to do the whole of the work, and 'as Mr. Stephens felt himself able to attend to them all, his salary was increased'.[31]

Samuel Stone, who knew the burden of official duties as well as anyone, told Stephens 'time after time that it was impossible for him to perform the whole of his work' and urged him to excuse himself from attendance at so many committee meetings.[32] Stephens, however, persistently refused to acknowledge the need to divide his duties, apparently finding the additional pay irresistible.

In June 1878 a more serious illustration of his growing incompetence occurred when some extensions of the filter beds at the sewage works collapsed shortly after their completion. Alderman Grimsley voiced the widespread belief that the accident would not have occurred if some other engineer had relieved Stephens of this work. 'It was', he said, 'perfectly impossible for Mr. Stephens, with the amount of work he had to do as Borough Surveyor, with the multifarious calls he had to make, with the number of inquiries he had to answer, with the constant attention he had to give to committees, and with all his other duties, to undertake works of that description—and so long as he remained on the Council he should certainly oppose Mr. Stephens having anything to do with any works outside his office as Borough Surveyor'.[33] In the words of Alderman Kempson, Stephens 'had brought it all on himself because he undertook more than he could accomplish', and he trusted that in future 'the great works of the Corporation would be left to proper men to carry out'.[34]

Stephens was spared further public exposure of his incompetence when he died, still at work, three years later. His successor, Joseph Gordon, was appointed at £700, the Council wisely insisting that he be engaged on a full-time basis.[35]

Extending the Borough Boundaries

It was the engineering works of the borough and in particular the provision of improved sewerage that prompted a move to extend the borough boundary in 1885. Proposals to extend the limits of Leicester had been made for many years as the fields around it filled with houses and the villages on its outskirts were sucked into the body of the town itself. A. J. Mundella, the Leicester-born hosier and prominent politician recalled in 1876 how 'as a child, he caught minnows in the purling stream that used to flow under the Willow Bridge; he swam in the old Soar when it was an unpolluted stream; he caught butterflies and entomological specimens with Henry Bates . . . in green lanes and on the Spinney Hills, where now he saw a town covering the fields and tall chimneys displacing the spreading elms'.[36] Ten years later Mundella would have found the relentless advance of brick and mortar even more destructive of those green lanes and fields. The *Leicester Chronicle* recalled, in similar vein, the days when villages like Knighton lay well out in the country, to be reached only by a long walk or a vehicle of some kind, whereas, by 1875, it was difficult to say where the town ended and the suburban village began.[37] For sanitary purposes, said the *Chronicle*, all these villages should come within the borough. The town had grown from just under 40,000 people in 1841 to 95,220 in 1871, and increased to 122,376 in another 10 years. The old boundaries fixed in 1835 were as unsuited to Leicester in 1886 as those of the medieval town had been in the days of William IV.

Proposals to extend the limits of the borough had been made for a number of years. The most radical proposal emanated from the Conservatives in 1867 when they proposed the absorption of Anstey, Belgrave, Blaby, Enderby, Humberstone, Knighton, Oadby, Thurmaston and Wigston.[38] A more modest suggestion came from Canon Vaughan, when as Chairman of the School Board he proposed in 1872 the annexation of New Parks, Belgrave, Beaumont Leys and Knighton.[39] The Council itself discussed extensions as early as 1880,[40] and the decision to promote a parliamentary Bill for this object was taken in July 1885. The borough sought to increase its size by over half its existing acreage and to take most of Belgrave, Knighton, Humberstone and Aylestone. A poll of the town on this issue produced a heavy vote in favour: 14,037 to 6,579 against the proposal.[41]

The *Leicester Journal* on the other hand had dismissed the idea in 1882, saying' 'a more absurd idea could scarcely be entertained by a maniac', and when the Bill failed to gain parliamentary approval, it waxed indignant at the waste of money entailed. 'The mania for spending money on anything, is delightfully fresh and juvenile, but, alas! we are not schoolboys'.[42]

The abortive Bill of 1886 cost the Corporation altogether £4,668 9s. 9d., and some recrimination was to be expected. The Conservative, William Millican, attacked Councillor Thomas Wright, the chief advocate of the Bill, in such terms that the Chamber was described as 'becoming a bear garden'.[43] Wright himself blamed the failure of the Bill on the Corporation's legal counsel, who were rarely on hand at the right time. John Storey suggested in retrospect that had the Beaumont Leys scheme and the new sewers prepared by Gordon been further advanced, the Bill might have fared better: 'At any rate', said Storey, 'this sewerage and sewage disposal question proved to be the weak point in an otherwise fairly good case'.[44]

From the ratepayers' viewpoint inclusion in the borough had much to recommend it. Leicester's rate had declined from 5s. 4d. to 4s. 10d. from 1882 to 1885 respectively, while those of Belgrave for example, had risen from 1s. 11d. in 1877 to 5s. 6d. in 1882, and remained at 5s. 5d. by 1885.[45] By 1890 memorials from the parishes of Aylestone, Humberstone and Evington urged the Council once again to seek an extension.[46] This time the borough prepared its ground more carefully, negotiating with the various authorities concerned as far as possible beforehand.

Indeed, according to the *Leicester Chronicle,* circumstances had arisen which induced some of the residents of suburban villages 'almost to clamour for the advantages of inclusion'.[47] Former opponents on the Borough Council had been largely won over, only three members voting against Alderman Wright's proposal.

Practical opposition to the scheme again rested on doubts as to the efficiency of the sewage scheme, but on this occasion the Commons Committee were satisfied that progress had been made. The only condition made in approving the Bill was that the Corporation should deal with its sewage efficiently and effectually cleanse the Soar within six months. Fears of loss of rateable value on the part of the new County Council led to a last-minute settlement, the borough giving the county £1,500 for two years to compensate its loss. In addition the Borough reduced the area to be taken on the fringes of the proposed extension and excluded the old village of Humberstone.[48]

The Bill thus passed the House of Lords Committee as an unopposed measure and received Royal Assent on 3 July 1891. Anticipating the success of the extension scheme, the Council had chosen the octogenarian, William Kempson, a hosiery manufacturer who was the son-in-law of John Flower, the local artist, as Mayor in 1890.[49] Already elected as Mayor in 1874, Kempson presided as the oldest chief magistrate in the country over the extension of the borough.

The absorption of Aylestone, Knighton, Belgrave and West Humberstone in 1891 complicate the study of the decennial census figures for Leicester. However, the town was by this time physically merging into its environs and it would be quite unrealistic to subtract the population of the suburban villages in order to make a true comparison with earlier decades. The enlarged borough of 1891 contained 42 per cent. more people than the old town of 1881, but the addition by 1901 was only 12.5 per cent., which suggests that population pressure had eased off by the end of the reign.[50]

Extending the Role of the Corporation

Between 1841 and 1901 there was a tenfold increase in the population, including the parts absorbed under the extension of 1891. A corollary of this unprecedented growth was the broader range of interests and activity of the Town Council. To policing and public health had been added the provision of publicly-owned gas, electricity and water supplies; baths, libraries, housing and technical education.

The extension of municipal control was sometimes a response to the prompting of officials, as in the original appointment of the town's medical officers in 1846, or the appointment of Mrs. Hartshorn as health visitor in 1895. Where large outlays of capital were involved, however, the impetus toward municipal action usually came from the central government, for local councillors were unwilling to invite the wrath of ratepayers unless the promised benefits were obvious to all.

Thus it was by initiative from Westminster that the borough police force was formed in 1836. Costing over £3,000 a year, it was the heaviest item in the Corporation's expenditure for many years.[51] Among locally-initiated undertakings, flood prevention works were the biggest recurrent drain on the resources of the town, while closely linked to these were the sewerage works carried out by Wicksteed and modified by successive borough surveyors. Here, however, it was a combination of local awareness of complex social and engineering problems together with the promptings of central government agencies that led to effective action.

Central government intervention in economic affairs was generally regarded with disapproval in the mid-Victorian period, apart from such acknowledged exceptions as the need to control child labour in mines and factories. It has been suggested, however, that belief in *laissez-faire* as a touchstone of government policy was less potent a force in the social sphere than in matters of commerce and industry.[52] While this is doubtless true on the national plane, there is little evidence in Leicester of such a distinction, nor is there much to suggest a progression toward collectivism before the mid '70s. Liberal opinion in Leicester was inclined by the mid-century to oppose collectivist measures *a priori* as conflicting with the philosophic concept of individual freedom. There was perhaps a reversion in Leicester away from the mood of the 1840s when the Town Council established a cemetery, a museum, a recreation ground, and came close to setting up a municipal water company. By the 1860s opinion seems to have hardened against such corporate action. Joseph Whetstone, once an advocate of municipal waterworks, argued that 'whatever was well done by private enterprise of individuals ought never to be attempted by the government'.[53] This seems to have been particularly the view in cultural matters. Alderman Collier expressed the Liberal's dilemma over the establishment of a municipal library: 'There was something so pleasant in the idea of a free library that he felt great difficulty in bringing his mind to oppose it', but on the other hand, 'he believed that in all matters of education, morality and religion the voluntary principle was the only sound principle'.[54]

Despite these reservations the Council resolved to establish a free library in 1862, and nine years later, largely through the persistent efforts of Alderman Stevenson, it acquired the old Mechanics' Institute and its library in Belvoir Street.[55] Branch libraries were provided through the generosity of two wealthy individuals, Israel Hart and Richard Harris, 20 years later, at Garendon Street and

Narborough Road. These benefactions did nothing to settle the controversy over Sunday opening of libraries, since Israel Hart made his grant on condition that the Garendon branch should open on the sabbath, and Richard Harris stipulated that his library should remain closed.[56]

When it purchased the gas and water works the Corporation was investing public money in highly profitable undertakings, but in buying the tramways it was taking on a service which had never brought its owners much reward. Founded in 1874 the company operated about 50 tramcars by 1888, as well as running horse-drawn omnibuses and providing vehicles for hire. The Corporation obtained powers to operate tramcars under an Act of 1890, and in 1900 it was evident that the company would either have to sell to the Corporation or find substantial new sources of capital. Before deciding on the purchase the Council appointed a special sub-committee to study Continental as well as British methods of operating tramways.[57] The report of this sub-committee favoured an electrified system, and in 1901, soon after the purchase of the company for £130,000, work began on the town's first generating station, at the Lero site on Belgrave Road.[58]

This was not the first time that deputations of councillors had undertaken fact-finding tours. There was, for instance, the sub-committee appointed to study the pail closet system of sewage removal in 1875. But the use of public funds to send councillors all over Europe was something quite new, and some less charitable observers saw such extravagance as reviving the spirit of the old Corporation with its junketings paid out of the rates. Councillor Walters, one of the deputation, sprang to his own defence with a summarised itinerary of the tour: '3,500 miles in fourteen days, with four nights in the train, journeying on one occasion for 24 hours at a stretch, and another 36, with the Borough Surveyor fetching one out of bed at six o'clock in the morning—on one morning at four—poking about for nine hours a day in tramway sheds, and endeavouring to understand Germans speaking English'. This, he said, was not his notion of a holiday.[59]

A Hint of Corruption

More serious were the charges levelled by the Socialist, George Banton, over dealings in land ripe for development. Banton maintained that several councillors were present at business meetings where their own interests were involved.[60] A committee set up to investigate the charges found that two Conservative councillors had bought land which was subsequently sold to the Corporation at a profit.

J. T. Biggs had bought property near the clock tower after the Corporation had declined to purchase it. But, said the committee, Biggs must have known that the property would soon be acquired in the course of road improvement, and he should therefore not have bought it. Biggs had also been a party to the sale of the old Huntingdon Tower—the medieval town house of the Earls of Huntingdon.[61] Although Biggs was exonerated by the committee, the suspicion remained as to whether he genuinely wanted to build on the land, or was out to make a quick profit by its resale to the Corporation. The committee had no doubt that this was the intention of another Conservative councillor, Frank Yearby, who had taken part in business meetings where he had a direct interest in the land under discussion. The committee concluded therefore by recording its 'very strong opinion that it is impolitic, unwise, and open to serious objection that any member of the Corporation should be found speculating in property on a well recognised line of street improvement, unless it be in the interest, or on behalf of the Corporation'.[62]

Measured against the more recent scandals of local government graft and corruption, it all seems rather small beer, but the issues of principle were recognised, and had the Banton committee's proposals been accepted at a national level, a good deal of subsequent jobbery would have been avoided.

Municipal Breathing Spaces

The unrestricted play of market forces on the land round Leicester created in the later 19th century acres of terraced housing with hardly any provision of open space. A small field had been set aside in 1839 for recreational use just south of the county gaol on Welford Road, but mid-19th-century Leicester was not well endowed with municipal parks and gardens. The old cricket ground in Wharf Street was sold and developed as building land in the early 1860s.[63] Danett's Hall and its ancient gardens suffered the same fate about the same time. A recreation ground on King Richard's Road near the West Bridge, opened in 1868, was sold in the mid '70s and provided a site for the first building put up by the School Board. Another recreation ground on the eastern side of the town was absorbed by the Great Northern Railway.[64]

A conviction seems to have taken root at Leicester that parks for pleasure and recreation were luxuries that ought to be provided by the munificence of private individuals and not at public expense. With the example of Joseph Strutt in Derby, who presented his town with a magnificent municipal park,[65] the Corporation of Leicester adopted a Micawberish attitude towards the subject, hoping that something would turn up through the generosity of some local philanthropist.

By 1878 it was becoming apparent that no such wealthy donor could be persuaded to make such a sacrifice, and several councillors asked why the Corporation should not take upon itself the responsibility of providing such places. Councillor Sladen added that 'he did not think it was very dignified that members of the Council of a rich town like Leicester should, cap in hand, ask for the gift of a park. Let them put their hands in their own pocket'.[66]

In fact, by 1878 the most imaginative step had already been taken in the establishment of Abbey Park. The opportunity for this venture arose out of the flood works approved in the Leicester Improvement Act of 1876, though the idea of a public park in this quarter had already been canvassed in the local press. An 'old inhabitant' had written urging the Council to provide some attraction at the Abbey ruins, such as a 'splendid botanical garden and winter gardens. Many a time', he wrote, 'I have observed strangers trudging through our streets, looking in vain for something fresh and novel, and after being tired in mind as well as body, sick and disgusted they get back to the Railway Station an hour or two before starting time, feeling sorry that they ever set their faces in the direction of Leicester'.[67]

The idea was taken up with enthusiasm by James Thompson in the *Chronicle*. The completion of the flood scheme in the Abbey meadows would, he said, provide just the right place for a peoples' park. Thompson elaborated on his vision: in the middle might be:

> 'A large pool or lakelet' while the soil thus excavated might be used 'to throw up earthen mounds and banks to diversify the surrounding surface with great success, and large masses of rock could be brought from no great distance to impart rustic boldness and fine effect to the landscape gardener's conception'.[68]

Thompson also suggested a cricket enclosure and an aviary as minor accessories to the grounds. The park was to be exactly as he imagined it. In 1882, five years after Thompson's death, Abbey Park was opened amid scenes of great pomp and ceremony by the Prince and Princess of Wales. It was peculiarly fitting that on that occasion they should have been presented with a volume of Thompson's *History of Leicester*.[69]

Victoria Park was not, by contemporary standards, a park at all. It was in fact the former racecourse, which happened to occupy part of the old southfields since the time of the enclosure award of 1804. There were moves to make it into a park with shrubbery and botanical gardens, but these came to nothing, and it remained a bare expanse of grassland where cricket was played and nursemaids flirted with young men while they took their charges for walks. It was indeed a rather shameful piece of wasteland and only a Leicester wag would dream of calling it Victoria Park.[70] So it was, however; the name stuck and tastes changed. The stylised rusticity of Abbey Park tends to pall, while the wide sweep of open grassland at the higher end of the town is one of its most cherished assets.

Spinney Hill Park was opened in 1886, its 36 acres having been sold at the moderate price of £18,000.[71] To the west of the town the 170 acres of the Mellor estate provided the largest of the municipal parks known as Western Park. It was bought, once again at a figure considerably below its market value, for £28,000 in 1897.[72] Even at this price one councillor objected to the expense when there was to be a new recreation ground opened on Fosse Road, nearer to the town centre. On this occasion Charles Bennion, soon to become head of the giant British United Shoe Machinery Corporation, spoke in favour of the purchase. The town would never regret it, he said.[73] Perhaps in this debate was born the seed of his great ambition, realised in 1928, by which he bought Bradgate Park, once the home of Lady Jane Grey, and donated it to the public.

One other recreation ground of importance was obtained in 1892 from St. Margaret's Vestry. This was 12 acres of the Parish Piece off Belgrave Road, near to the Melton turn. It was pressure from the Leicestershire Footpaths Association that resulted in much of this land being appropriated as a recreation ground and not sold for building. Part of it went to provide a new branch library and the Cossington Street baths, the largest covered swimming bath in the country at the time of its opening in 1897.[74]

The Rates and the Ratepayers

The cost of all these undertakings was not always borne by the ratepayers with equanimity. Robert Read in his *Modern Leicester,* published in 1881, castigated the formation of Abbey Park as 'our Corporation Folly' and declared that 'the very large expenditure going on and contemplated in that dank, diphtherial, and febrile spot' positively gave him 'the shivers'.[75]

Underlying the whole story of local government in Leicester in the 19th century was the debate about expenditure. From its inception in 1836 the new Council was determined to economise in the money raised from the ratepayers. A succession of Improvement Bills was suspended, truncated or pared down to avoid unnecessary expenditure, and always with the cry that the burgesses could not afford and would not consent to pay higher rates. It is a cry familiar enough in any age, but one wonders what substance the threat of defection at the polls had in reality. How far was there a real risk of defeat for the Liberals on this account?

Certainly there was plenty of evidence of public protest about the rates burden. Letters to the press, editorials and memorials from the ratepayers testify to the reluctance of the citizens to part with their money. The memorial signed by 186 ratepayers in 1856 spoke of 'exacting, unnecessary' increases in rates as 'an imposition which we are unwilling to pay'.[76] In 1869 the *Leicester Chronicle* reported several meetings of ratepayers which 'openly expressed their opinions in favour of an economical expenditure of public money, a more rigid oversight of that expenditure–of the postponement of the building of a Town Hall–and of the adoption of none but purely necessary local improvements'.[77] The *Leicester Chronicle* invariably took the view that the rates were unnecessarily high, observing in 1841; 'A town Council, which came into power on professions of the most rigorous economy, will not we think run the risk of being kicked out for an attempt upon the pockets of their constituents; and that this would be the instant result, no-one affects to doubt'.[78] The *Journal* dismissed the proposed Improvement Bill of that year as 'a pretty thing to read, certainly; and . . . a very nice specimen of moonshine'.[79] One correspondent of the *Leicester Chronicle* in 1845 observed that the town's ancient name 'Ratae Coritanorum' might again become appropriate–Ratae, the city of rates.[80]

But the rates burden did not enable the Conservatives to make any substantial inroad into the massive Liberal domination of the Council. This is partly explained by the memory of Tory mismanagement. The sins of 'the wicked old body' were visited on the Tory candidates unto the third and fourth generation. And when the policy of economy was cast to the winds in 1877, it was a Conservative, William Winterton, who led the crusade for civic spending.

When he was appointed as Chairman of the Highways and Sewerage Committee, Winterton reflected that he had 'probably disappointed the expectations of some gentlemen'.

TOTAL RATES IN THE POUND PER YEAR 1845 TO 1914

	s.	d.		s.	d.		s.	d.
1845		8	1869	3	0½	1893	4	10
1846		9	1870	3	2	1894	6	0
1847		10	1871	3	1	1895	5	4
1848		9	1872	3	2	1896	4	10
1849		9	1873	3	5	1897	4	8
1850	2	3	1874	4	0	1898	5	2
1851	1	10	1875	4	4	1899	5	3
1852	1	9	1876	4	6	1900	5	10
1853	2	4¾	1877	4	6	1901	5	10
1854	2	8¾	*1878	3	10	1902	5	11
1855	2	9¾	1879	4	2½	1903	5	9
1856	2	9¾	1880	4	0	1904	5	9
1857	2	11	1881	3	8	1905	5	6
1858	2	7¼	1882	3	6	1906	5	5
1859	2	5½	1883	3	10	1907	5	6
1860	2	7½	1884	4	4	1908	5	7
1861	2	7	1885	4	0	1909	5	8
1862	2	10½	1886	3	6	1910	5	11
1863	2	8¾	1887	3	2	1911	5	9½
1864	2	7¼	1888	4	2	1912	5	9½
1865	2	5½	1889	4	2	1913	5	11
1866	2	4¼	1890	4	0	1914	6	3
1867	2	8	1891	3	8			
1868	2	11½	1892	4	0			

*N.B.—Financial Year altered to end in March instead of August.

Note the rise in expenditure consequent upon the establishment of the Local Board of Health in 1849.

Instead of dealing with the finances of the Corporation in the Highways Committee in a penurious manner, with a view to cutting down the rates a penny or twopence in the pound, he, as plainly as he could, insisted that instead of making a saving they ought to expand somewhat more in widening the streets and in providing a better system of getting rid of the disastrous consequences that followed the floods in the town.[81] Winterton was an individualist and never representative of Conservative opinion generally, but in the late 19th century his views were echoed by another Conservative, who gained for himself the respect and trust of his political opponents.[82] William Wilkins

Vincent, who chaired the Finance Committee, predicted a rise in the rates for March 1897 as a consequence of expenditure on the new Swithland Reservoir and new road works and sewers. He admitted that the cost of all these would be worked off in a few years.

> 'But even then we shall not have reached finality', he said. 'There is no such thing as finality in municipal matters. Every year we aim at a higher standard of comfort in municipal affairs. Our sanitary and social demands increase, our educational needs tend upwards, and the growth of the town brings with it increasing responsibilities, and proportionately increased expenditure'.[83]

It was an astute and accurate comment on the progress of local government in the Victorian town.

When the cry of 'Down with the rates' was heard at the end of the reign it was more often the working-class spokesmen of the Independent Labour Party who voiced it most urgently. It was almost as if the early socialists associated municipal expenditure with corporate extravagance, like the Radicals of 1836. Thus, when the Council debated the establishment of the Art and Technical College in 1895, it was Councillor Richards of the Independent Labour Party who alone spoke against the scheme. 'Before they went in for science, or art and literature', he said, 'they wanted to see starving people fed'.[84] Even George Banton's determination to expose corruption can be seen as a reflection of the same concern for economy in municipal expenditure.

By contrast, it was often the Conservatives who made the running in urging greater public initiative and higher spending for corporate purposes. The role of Winterton in bringing water and gas under municipal control has been spelled out in detail, as has that of Councillor Richardson in proposing the first Council housing in Leicester. In 1895 another prominent Conservative, Sir Herbert Marshall, prompted the establishment of a municipal orchestra and put himself at the forefront of a renewed campaign to establish a town hall a few years later.[85]

It might be thought that the stern warnings of Joseph Whetstone and the economists were somewhat exaggerated, but a look at what happened elsewhere would suggest on the contrary that the economists' fears were only too real. E. P. Hennock made a study of the course of events in Birmingham and Leeds, where similar debates took place between Improvers and Economists.[86] He recounts Birmingham's attempt to raise money for improvement in 1855 which led to the formation of a Ratepayers' Protection Society. The result of its activities was the resignation of the town clerk and of the entire Finance and Public Works Committee, and the replacement of the borough surveyor by his assistant at half his salary. Within the space of seven years the representation of big businessmen on the Corporation fell by half and its deliberations became dominated by petty shopkeepers intent on reducing the rates burden. At Leeds the Corporation, which showed admirable promise after 1835, remained in the van of progress until 1842. In that year, however, conflict over an Improvement Bill led to a similar reaction and a gradual withdrawal into the politics of parsimony. Hennock concludes that, 'Only a Council which devised means wherewith to ward off a ratepayers' reaction would survive to carry out effective improvements over a long period'.[87]

The Changing Composition of the Council

When the Liberal hegemony finally crumbled in Leicester, it was not so much from defection to the Tories, as from the emergence of the Labour Party with its claim to be the true champion of working-class interests. The widening of the municipal franchise in 1869 thus spelled the beginning of a long but inevitable decline in the fortunes of the Liberal Party.

The men who debated Corporation policy at the turn of the century did not in their politics and social standing differ markedly from the first generation of radical councillors. A comparison of the membership in 1836 with that in 1902 reveals the continued dominance of the Liberal Party, over two-thirds being within its ranks. Fourteen of the 64 councillors and aldermen listed here were engaged in professional occupations: four solicitors,

OCCUPATIONS AND POLITICAL AFFILIATION OF COUNCILLORS, 1836, 1902, and 1914

Occupations	1836	1902	1914
Professions			
Solicitor		4 (2C)	3 (3C)
Doctor	3	4 (1C)	4 (1C)
Architect		3	1
Accountant/Actuary		2	2 (1C)
Surveyor	1		1 C
Textile Manufacture and Allied Trades			
Hosier	19	2 (1C)	1
Woolstapler	1		
Wool/Worsted Spinner	3		
Dyer	1	1	1
Hat Manufacturer		1 C	1 C
Framework Knitter/Hosiery Machinist			2 (1S)
Elastic Web Manufacturer		2 (1C)	1
Footwear Industry			
Boot and Shoe Manufacturer/Factor		9	7 (2C, 1S)
Boot/Shoe Operative		2 (2S)	3 (3S)
Banker	3 (1C)		
Gentleman	6	4 (2C)	2 (1C)
Wholesale Traders			
Grocer		2	1
Confectioner		1	1 C
Fruiterer		1	
Tobacco Importer			1 C
Retail Traders			
Wine Merchants		2 (2 C)	2 (2C)
Grocer	4	1	1
Baker	1		2
Chemist	1		
Corn Merchant/Dry Salter		2 (1C)	1
Coal Merchant		2 (1S)	2 (1S)
Butcher		2	1
Ironmonger		1	
Draper	3 (1C)	3 (1C)	2 (2C)
Other Business Interests/Employment			
Ironfounder	1	1	1
Builder		1 C	1
Coach Builder	1 C		

Occupations and Political Affiliation, etc.—*continued*—

Occupations	1836	1902	1914
Other Business Interests, etc.—*continued*			
Carpet Warehouseman		1	
Cabinet Maker	1		
Cycle Maker			1 S
Malster	1	1 C	1
Photographer		1	
Carrier	4 (1C)		
Brazier	1		
Sanitary Engineer		1 C	
Painter/Decorator		1	
Superintendent Registrar		1	1
Musician..		1	
Cashier			1 C
Secretary			1
T.U. Official		1 S	2 (2S)
Dental Mechanic			1 S
Shopfitter/Joiner			2 (1S)
P.O. Clerk			1 S
Factory Manager			1
Agent		1 S	1 S
Printer/Publisher	1	2	3 (1 S)
Print Operative			1 S

Liberal	52	44	30
Conservative	4	15	18
Socalist	—	5	16

Numbers given in brackets refer to Liberal Unionists and Conservatives (C) and Socialist or Lib.-Lab. (S).

four doctors, three architects, an actuary, an accountant, and the Superintendent Registrar who belongs more properly to this group than to the clerical and artisan section, in which is included a T.U. official with a shoe operative and an engineer's fitter. A couple of Liberals and a brace of Tories still presented themselves as 'gentlemen'. With two wine merchants represented, as against one maltster of Liberal persuasion, the drink trade remained predominantly the preserve of the Conservatives. The strongest single trade represented was that of boot and shoe manufacture, where all 10 were Liberals in 1902, apart from the Lib.-Lab. operative mentioned above. Among the 21 representatives of other commercial and industrial interests were two elastic web manufacturers who, like the two hosiery manufacturers, were shared equally by the two major parties.

In the next decade, however, fundamental changes came over the composition of the Council. The Liberals lost their overall majority in 1909 and by 1912 Labour had taken 14 seats, barely less than the Conservatives who had sixteen. Despite an ephemeral supremacy in 1928, however, it was not until 1945 that an effective socialist majority was elected.

As R. Clements found in his study of municipal politics at Bristol, the wealthiest businessmen tended to cut themselves off from local politics in the 20th century,[88] though the lament that the Council lacked men of calibre it once enjoyed was by no means new.[89] What appears to have happened in Bristol and Leicester was the broadening of the Council to represent a wider spectrum of interests and classes, though the timing of this seems to have been somewhat later in Leicester, and it was indistinguishable from the growth of influence of the Labour party.

The extended franchise, effective Trade Unionism, more widespread literacy and ease of communication, and, above all, the spread of socialist ideas, led working men in the later years of the 19th century to become aware of their own identity as a class, with interests different from and to some extent opposed to those of capital. For some years Trade Unionists had been elected to the Town Council as working men's candidates, and the School Board also welcomed a working man to its ranks in 1871.[90] The working men generally sided with the Liberals, and by 1890 Liberal-Labour candidates were being elected to the Council and to the School Board.

By 1893, however, more militant sections of the Labour movement founded the Independent Labour Party, and it soon had a following in Leicester.[91] In the parliamentary election of that year the I.L.P. candidate polled over 4,000 votes, while the Liberal got in with a margin of only 217 over his Conservative opponents, and in the General Election of 1895 this was down to less than 100 votes. It was this knife-edge situation which led to the success of the Conservative, Sir John Rolleston, in 1900, and to the pact in 1903 between Herbert Gladstone, the Liberal Chief Whip and J. Ramsey Macdonald, the I.L.P. candidate for Leicester, whereby the Liberals agreed to field only one candidate, while Macdonald took the other seat for Labour.[92]

Reaction to the socialist bid for working-class votes changed from a rather condescending encouragement to one of alarm at the consequences of a split vote. In 1895 when the I.L.P. won a third place on the municipal Council the *Leicester Chronicle* informed its readers: 'They cannot do any harm, of course, but if they take their share of the work, and are willing to be guided by experience, their ideas will be broadened. For the present they represent a body of opinion that should not be ignored, though it is crude and ill-informed'.[93] By 1909 Liberals were openly urged to vote for the I.L.P. candidate in Aylestone ward, no Liberal opposing him.[94]

Even before the Home Rule split there was a prevalent disillusion among supporters of the Liberal Party. Discontent with Gladstone's second ministry of 1880–84 led to outspoken criticism by P. A. Taylor, the senior Leicester Liberal member. Taylor opposed the use of the closure motion to silence Irish obstruction in parliament and voted against his own party on the issue. Defending him against subsequent criticism, the Rev. J. Page Hopps of the Great Meeting recalled that Gladstone's only achievements up to that time were 'blundering coercion bills for Ireland, Jingo fighting in Egypt, and very questionable gagging resolutions in the House of Commons'; hardly, as he pointed out, 'the measures which should be elevated into tests of soundness in the faith'.[95] Taylor himself declared that expediency was 'eating out the very vitals of the national character', and that he would rather see the return of a Tory ministry than sanction the degradation of parliament.[96]

In the light of its internal frictions, the Home Rule issue can almost be seen as gratifying a death-wish in the party;

the cross of Irish Home Rule serving to resurrect Gladstone as the undying symbol of Liberal idealism. Francis Hewitt sang his praises in an editorial on the 'Glamour of a Name'. 'Mr. Gladstone has made us Home Rulers', he wrote, and he asked if future ages would dream of 'comparing the wavering Salisbury, the shifty Churchill, . . . the self-conscious Chamberlain, with this heroic old man, who almost single-handed, with one foot in the grave, has undertaken the most daring task of his eventful and stirring career, and is carrying it through with a force of knowledge, genius, and energy sufficient to make the political fortune of a dozen ordinary statesmen?' The Home Rule Bill was defeated, but said Hewitt: 'We decline to sing its requiem. The Imperial Parliament is not omnipotent. It has worked its present will; but it has merely ended the First Act of an august drama which is destined to a triumphant finale'.[97]

A number of the wealthiest and most prominent supporters of the Leicester Liberal party followed Chamberlain and Bright into alliance with the Conservatives over Home Rule: among them were Alderman Thomas Wright, the Faire brothers, T. Fielding Johnson, and Canon Vaughan. For some time it was hoped a reconciliation could be effected, for the Unionists still felt themselves to be Liberals rather than Conservatives. Alderman Wright could not bring himself to stand as a parliamentary candidate in 1892, when the Conservatives sought to select him as their man. Two years later Wright announced his reconciliation with the Liberal party, but after little over a year he was again siding with the Tories and by 1899 he was a full member of the Conservative Constitution Club.[99]

Radical Leicester had its roots firmly planted in the puritanism of the Great Meeting, but by the end of the 19th century many of the prominent members of that body had gone over to the Established Church, and some had married into county society, sent their sons to public schools, and settled down to enjoy their wealth rather than exert themselves greatly to increase it. In contrast to Joseph Whetstone, who declined a knighthood in 1837, several leading Liberals of the late 19th century accepted honours, if, indeed, they did not actively seek them.[89]

But if radical nonconformity had declined, the traditions of probity and unselfish service to the town lived on. The significance of the charges levelled by George Banton in 1897 lies not so much in any evidence of corruption brought to light, as in the general assumption that service to the community requires patent moral rectitude. The minor indiscretions of Messrs. Biggs and Yearby served only to underline that fact. If a passionate young Socialist like Banton could find little of which to complain in the conduct of civic affairs in Leicester, others were inclined to be more generous. One Liberal councillor on his retirement after 20 years' service, wrote of his respect for the members of the Corporation in these words: 'I remember when I was a young man I held the young man's cynical faith that all governing bodies were tied up with red tape, and existed as much for personal as for public benefit. I have learnt in the Leicester Council Chamber to utterly renounce that foolish faith. I have found there a representative body almost ideal in its calm wisdom, its incorruptibility, its forward policy, and its absolute devotion to the best interests of the town. Old England cannot go far wrong while its Town and County Councils follow the lead of Leicester'.[100]

REFERENCES

Abbreviations used

H.B. Hall Books of the Corporation of Leicester.
H.S. Minutes of the Highways and Sewerage Committee.
L.C. *Leicester Chronicle.*
L.J. *Leicester Journal.*
L.R.O. Leicester Record Office.
M.O. Reports of the Medical Officer of Health.
T.L.A.S. Transactions of the Leicester Archaeological and Historical Society.
V.C.H. *Victoria County History of Leicestershire.*

Preface

1. J. L. Hammond, 'The Social Background' in *A Century of Municipal Progress,* edited by Laski, Jennings and Robson (1935), p. 37.

Introduction

1. S. and B. Webb, *English Local Government,* Vol. 4 'Statutory Authorities for Special Purposes' (1922), p. 353, *et seq.*
2. J. B. Black, *The Reign of Elizabeth, 1558-1603* (1936), p. 175 says of the Justice of the Peace that 'he was the beast of burden on whose broad shoulders the government continually devolved new tasks'.
3. S. and B. Webb, *op. cit.,* Vol. 4, p. 479.
4. Elie Halevy, *Before 1835,* in Laski, *et al.,* p. 33.
5. E. J. Hobsbawm and George Rude, *Captain Swing* (1969).
6. Modern historians take a more appreciative view of the system. *See* Mark Blaugh, 'The Myth of the Old Poor Law and the Making of the New', *Journal of Economic History,* XXIII (1963), p. 151–84; D. A. Baugh, 'The Cost of Poor relief in South-East England, 1790–1834', *Economic History Review,* 2nd Series, Vol. XXVIII, No. 1, February 1975, pp. 50-68.
7. Baugh, *op. cit.,* p. 50.
8. *The Works of Jeremy Bentham,* ed. J. Bowring, Vol. IX, Russell and Russell, New York (1962), p. 640.

9. M. W. Flinn, *Introduction to Chadwick's Report on the Sanitary Conditions of the Labouring Population of Great Britain, 1842* (1965), p. 32. Professor Flinn comments: 'It is hardly possible to overestimate the value of the work done by the medical officers in the service of the poor law in the 1830s. Almost every page of the Sanitary Report bears ample testimony to their hard work, conscientiousness, experience, medical commonsense, and compassion. Their knowledge and experience of the factors affecting the lives, work, and health of the working class provided an inexhaustible mine from which the fires of agitation and propaganda might be stoked'.

10. Halevy, *op. cit.*, p. 34.

11. S. and B. Webb, *op. cit.*, Vol. 3, *The Manor and the Borough* (1908), pp. 714–21.

12. *Ibid.*, p. 734.

13. *Report of the Commission on Municipal Corporations in England and Wales*, reprinted in British Parliamentary Papers, Government Municipal Corporations, 2, Session 1835, Irish University Press, p. 46.

14. *Ibid.*, p. 49.

15. *Ibid.*, p. 17.

16. Statutes of the Realm 1835, Cap. 76, section XCII.

17. *Ibid.*, Cap. 50, section VI.

18. Jean Toft, unpublished thesis on 'Public Health in Leeds in the Nineteenth Century: A Study in the Growth of Local Government Responsibility, *c.* 1815-1850'. M.A. Thesis, University of Manchester 1966. p. 62.

19. These were: the Street Commissioners, the Deritend and Bordesley Commissioners, the Duddeston and Nechells Commissioners, the Surveyors of Highways for Deritend, Bordesley and Edgbaston, and the Council itself, created under the Municipal Corporations Act in 1838.

20. J. T. Bunch, *History of the Corporation of Birmingham*, Vol. I, p. 338.

21. S. and B. Webb, *op. cit.*, Vol. 4, p. 274.

22. *Ibid.*, p. 348.

23. *Ibid.*, p. 349.

24. This figure is calculated from those in Mitchell and Deane *Abstract of British Historical Statistics* (1971), p. 24. Asa Briggs in his *Victorian Cities* (1968), gives somewhat different figures and puts the percentage increase for the decade at 65.5.

25. *Report on Modes of Treating Town Sewage*, P.P. (1876), XXXVIII, p. xvi, quoted by M. W. Flinn, *Public Health Reform in Britain* (1968), p. 18.

26. R. A. Lewis, *Edwin Chadwick and the Public Health Movement 1832 to 1854* (1952), p. 22.

27. M. W. Flinn, *Public Health Reform in Britain*, p. 27.

28. *Ibid.*, p. 29–30.

29. S. E. Finer, *The Life and Times of Sir Edwin Chadwick* (1952), p. 298.

30. *Ibid.*, p. 211.

31. *Ibid.*,p. 235.

32. Duncan Gray, *Nottingham through 500 Years* (1960), pp. 193-4.

33. Finer, *op. cit.*, p. 241-2.

34. Asa Briggs, 'Cholera and Society', *Past and Present* (1961), p. 85-6;

35. *L.C.*, 19 November 1831.

36. *Ibid.*

37. Lewis, *op. cit.*, p. 42.

38. M. W. Flinn, *op. cit.*, p. 33.

39. *Ibid.*, p. 34.

40. Royston Lambert, *Sir John Simon, 1816-1904* (1963), p. 231, *et seq.*

41. Gray, *op. cit.*, p. 194

42. *Ibid. loc. cit.*

43. Minutes of the Local Government Board at Hinckley, 11 February 1868.

44. *Ibid.*, p. 4, 1873.

45. Unpublished M.A. thesis by A. J. Archer, 'A Study in Local Sanitary Administration in Certain Selected Areas, 1846-1875'. University of Wales (1967), *passim.*

46. A. P. Stewart and E. Jenkins, *The Medical and Legal Aspects of Sanitary Reform,* with an introduction by M. W. Flinn. Reprinted in the Victorian Library of the Leicester University Press, 1969.

47. Archer, *op. cit.*, p. 253, P.R.O. M.H. 13/239 letter to Local Government Act Offices, 30 May 1868.

48. *Ibid.*, p. 255, P.R.O. M.H. 13/239 Arnold Taylor to Local Government Act Office, July 1868.

49. Hammond, *op. cit.*, p. 48.

50. Halevy, *op. cit.*, p. 36.

51. Hammond, *op. cit.*, pp. 51-2.

52. J. Redlich and F. Hirst, *Local Government in England*, Vol. I (1903), p. 211.

Chapter One

1. Thomas Baskerville ref. in J. Simmons's *Leicester Past and Present,* Vol. I, p. 95. Simmons refers to Historical MSS Commission, Portland, ii, 308-9.

2. Newspaper cutting in Wakerley's scrapbook dated 17 July 1921.

3. Susanna Watts, *A Walk through Leicester* (1969).

4. William Gardiner, *Music and Friends or Pleasant Recollections of a Dilletante*, 3 vols. (1837), Vol. I, p. 89.

5. *Ibid.*, Vol. III, p. 11.

6. R. A. Church, *Economic and Social Change in a Midland Town, Victorian Nottingham, 1815-1900* (1966), p. 8; J. Prest, *The Industrial Revolution in Coventry* (1960), p. 34.

7. Watts, *op. cit.*, p. 76.

8. Thomas Cooper, *Life of Thomas Cooper* (1872), p. 141.

9. Report on the Conditions of Framework Knitters, P.P. 1845.

10. Census Returns 1851 and 1861 for Leicester.

11. *Ibid.*, 1851, Vol. II:ii, p. 588.

12. *Ibid.*, 1861, Vol. II, p. 588.

13. *Ibid.*, 1871, Vol. III, p. 390.

14. J. Buck, Address to the Leicester Literary and Philosophical Society, 1867.

15. Joseph Dare, Volume of Annual Reports to the Leicester Domestic Mission Society, 1846 to 1877. Report for 1847, p. 5.

16. *Ibid.*, 1848, p. 10.

17. *Ibid.*, 1849, p. 6.

18. *Ibid.*, 1850, p. 5.

19. *Ibid.*, 1851, p. 4–5.

20. *Ibid.*, 1852, p. 6.

21. *Ibid.*, 1853, p. 7.

22. *Ibid.*, 1854, p. 4.

23. *Ibid.*, 1858, p. 7.

24. *Ibid.*, 1860, p. 5–6.

25. Prest, *op. cit.*, 119 and 121.

26. *V.C.H. Northampton*, Vol. 2, p. 327 and Note supplied by the Registrar General in the Census Report of 1871, p. 344: 'About the year 1861 the strike at Northampton caused the removal of a large portion of its shoe trade to Leicester, and the depression at Coventry a year or two later brought a large number of ribbon weavers from that city and neighbourhood who were absorbed by the elastic web trade'. *But see* J. Simmons, *op. cit.*, Vol. 2, pp. 2–3. He discounts the effect of the strikes since mechanised shoe production had already begun in Leicester. The strike at Northampton was at most a contributory factor and not a causal one.

27. A. T. Patterson, *Radical Leicester* (1954), p. 388.

28. Dare Report for 1862, p. 11–12.

29. *Ibid.*, 1863, p. 3–4.

30. *Ibid.*, 1865, p. 7, 1872, p. 5.

31. Cooper, *op. cit.*, p. 142.

32. Dare Report for 1876, p. 8.

33. I. C. Ellis, *Records of Nineteenth Century Leicester* (1953), p. 39.

34. Simmons, *op. cit.*, Vol. P156. The price of coal fell by 45 per cent. from 16s. to 11s. a ton.

35. Colin Ellis, *The History of Ellis and Everard Ltd., and Joseph Ellis and Sons Ltd.* (1924), pp. 9–11.

36. *L.C.*, 6 December 1879.

37. *L.C.*, 5 February 1853; *see V.C.H.*, Vol. 4, p. 206.

38. R. H. Evans, *The Biggs Family of Leicester*, T.L.A.S., Vol. XLVIII (1972–3), p. 32.

39. *Ibid.* 33, Thomas Corah was in fact a member of the Council from 1863 to 1868.

40. C. W. Webb, *An Historical Record of Nathaniel Corah and Sons Ltd.*, p. 34, printed privately for Corah's.

41. *L.C.*, 6 January 1883.

42. 'Goddard's of Leicester' in *Histories of Famous Firms* (1956), produced by the British Bulletin of Commerce, and published by the Aldwych Press, p. 2.

43. *Ibid.*

44. Thomas Cook, *Temperance Jubilee Celebrations at Leicester and Market Harborough* (1886), p. 3. (In Leicester Reference Library.)

45. *Ibid.*, p. 27.

46. J. Simmons, *Thomas Cook of Leicester*, T.L.A.S. Vol. XLIX (1973-4), p. 27.

47. *L.C.*, 21 June 1884.

48. G. T. Rimmington, M.A. Thesis, University of Leicester 1959 on *The Historical Geography of the Engineering Industry in Leicester*, p. 137.

49. *Ibid.*, p. 138; *see also* Simmons *Leicester Past and Present*, Vol. I, p. 132, and Vol. II, pp. 4–5.

50. *Leicester Mercury*, 29 April 1854 (cutting inserted in Minutes of the Leicester Secular Society in L.R.O.).

51. Sidney Gimson, *Random Recollections of the Leicester Secular Society* (1932 and 1935), Vol. I, p. 23, in L.R.O.

52. W. S. F. Pickering, 'The Religious Census–a Useless Experiment?' *British Journal of Sociology* (1967), p. 402.

53. *The Religious Census of 1851*, P.P. 1852–53, reprinted in Irish University Press series, Vol. CCLXI.

54. *L.J.*, 22 June 1877.

55. J. Simmons, *Life in Victorian Leicester* (1971), pp. 74–5.

56. *L.C.*, 20 April 1878, and W. Y. Fullerton, *Memoir of F. B. Meyer* in City Reference Library.

57. R. Read, *Modern Leicester* (1880).

58. *L.C.*, 12 February 1881.

59. *Ibid.*

Chapter Two

1. S. and B. Webb, *op. cit.*, Vol. 3, *The Manor and the Borough*, p. 476.

2. *Ibid. loc. cit.*

3. A. Temple Patterson, *Radical Leicester* (1954), p. 141–2.

4. S. and B. Webb, *op. cit.*, p. 478.

5. *Report of Municipal Corporations Commission*, 1835, Vol. III, p. 1909.

6. Patterson, *op. cit.*, p. 193.

7. *Ibid.*, p. 155.

8. H.B., 24 March 1829. Patterson incorrectly gives the figure as 4½ per cent.

9. Patterson, *op. cit.*, pp. 212, 218–19.

10. H.B. 22 December 1835.

11. *Ibid.*, 24 December 1835.

12. *L.J.*, 25 December 1835.

13. *Ibid.*

14. *Ibid.*

15. *L.J.*, 1 January 1836.

16. E. P. Hennock, 'Finance and Politics in Urban Local Government in England, 1835–1900', *Historical Journal*, VI, 2 (1963), p. 217.

17. Patterson, *op. cit.*, pp. 214–5; the remaining member was a Huntingdonian, i.e., a follower of the sect which owed its origin to the Methodist leanings of the Countess of Huntingdon.

18. J. Throsby, *History of Leicester* (1791), p. 380.

19. *V.C.H.*, IV, p. 251.

20. *L.J.*, 22 January 1836; *see also* W. Kelly, *The Great Mace of Leicester* (1875).

21. Town Clerk's correspondence for 22 March 1837 in the L.R.O.

22. *Ibid. See* letters in 25 March 1836 and 26 May 1836 for Stone's reply.

23. H.B., 19 August 1836.

24. Town Clerk's correspondence 19 October 1837.

25. *L.C.*, 27 June 1874, letter from 'Vindex'; R. W. Greaves, *The Corporation of Leicester, 1689–1836* (1939), p. 138. 'Vindex' was the pen-name of James Thompson, according to Lawrence Brown. (*See* L. Brown, *The Revenge of the Whigs*, p. 19, in pamphlet collection at Leicester Reference Library.)

26. E. P. Hennock, *Fit and Proper Persons–Ideal and Reality in Nineteenth Century Urban Government*, (1973).

27. *Ibid.*

28. James Thompson, *The History of Leicester in the Eighteenth Century* (1871), p. 186.

29. *L.C.*, 28 August 1840.

30. *L.J.*, 22 February 1849.

31. H.B., 25 August 1841.

32. *L.C.*, 21 September 1844.

33. *Short History of Leicester* (1879); *History of Leicester in the Eighteenth Century* (1849); and *An Essay on English Municipal History* (1867).

34. H.B., 21 May 1845.

35. *L.C.*, 1 November 1845.

36. H.B., 23 July 1845.

37. Finer, *op. cit.*, p. 242.
38. H.B., 10 November 1845.
39. *L.C.*, 25 October 1845.
40. *L.C.*, 31 January 1846.
41. *L.C.*, 2 January 1847 and 23 January 1847.
42. *L.C.*, 20 March 1847.
43. The Nuisances Removal Act, 1846, Cap. 96.
44. Patterson, *op. cit.*, p. 74.
45. H.B., 22 January 1840; Goodyer's obituary, *L.C.*, 30 September 1876. Bown resigned his post as Accountant in March 1849. *See also* T.L.A.S. Vol. LI (1975-6), article by Clifford Stanley, p. 15.
46. *L.J.*, 13 September 1850.
47. H.B., 7 October 1846.
48. H.B., 28 October 1846.
49. *L.C.*, 1 January 1881.
50. Lambert, *op. cit.*, pp. 109, 113–4.
51. *Ibid.*, p. 144.
52. H.B., 24 February 1847.
53. *Ibid*,
54. *Ibid.*
55 *Ibid.*
56. *Ibid.*
57. Stewart and Jenkins, *op. cit.*, p. 80–1.
58. *L.J.*, 17 January 1868.

Chapter Three

1. Chadwick to Lyon Playfair, quoted in R. A. Lewis, *Edwin Chadwick and the Public Health Movement 1832 to 1854* (1952), p. 4.
2. Minutes Book of Leicester Guardians, 6 December 1836, in L.R.O.
3. *Ibid.*, 16 July 1839.
4. Patterson, *op. cit.*, p. 227.
5. *Ibid. loc. cit.*
6. *Ibid.*, p. 228.
7. H.B., 19 May 1847.
8. H.B., 1 March 1848.
9. *Ibid.*
10. H.B., 22 March 1848, and *L.J.*, 14 April 1848.
11. H.B., 22 March 1848.
12. William Ranger report to the General Board of Health on the town of Leicester, 1849, p. 8.
13. *Ibid.*, p. 11.
14. P.R.O. MH5, letter from Ranger to Chadwick, 25 January 1849; correspondence of General Board of Health.
15. H.B., 27 July 1849.

16. *Ibid. loc. cit.*

17. P.P. 1844, First Report of Health of Towns Commission, p. 263.

18. Town Clerk's correspondence, 1849/50, Letters 42 and 43 in L.R.O.

19. William Farr, letter to Registrar General in Second Annual Report of the Registrar General, 1840, pp. 84–5.

20. P.P. 1854, Microfilm car. Vol. xxxv, pp. 1–99, c. 34.

21. Thomas Wicksteed, *Preliminary Report upon the Sewerage, Drainage and Supply of Water for the Borough of Leicester* (1850), p. 20.

22. 'Report of the Highways and Sewerage Committee of the Local Board of Health for the Borough of Leicester, respecting the proposed scheme for the sewerage of Leicester and the report of the General Board of Health thereon, with (1) A report from Mr. Lee, one of the Superintending Inspectors of the General Board of Health; (2) A letter from the General Board to the Local Board; and (3) The reply of Mr.Wicksteed to the Report of Mr. Lee' (1852), iv.

23. *Ibid.*, p. v.

24. *Ibid.*, p. vi.

25. *Ibid.*, p. 6.

26. *Ibid.*, p. 12.

27. *Ibid. loc. cit.*

28. *L.C.*, 4 September 1852.

29. *L.C.*, 5 August 1854.

30. *See* reference 17 above.

31. Flinn, *Public Health Reform in Britain*, p. 46.

32. Public Health Act, 1848, Cap. LXIII.

33. John Storey, *Historical Sketch of some of the Principal Works and Undertakings of the Council at the Borough of Leicester* (1895), p. 104.

34. P.R.O. MH13, Report by William Ranger, 18 February 1851.

35. *Ibid.*, letter from John Windley and Thomas Cooper, 25 February 1851.

36. E. Chadwick, *Sewer Manure*, Report to the Metropolitan Sewers Commission (1849).

37. H.S., 21 July 1855.

38. *L.C.*, 2 October 1852.

39. P.P. 1853, Enquiry into the prevalence of Disease at Croydon and to the Plan of Sewerage, p. 89.

40. H.S., 18 September 1857 and 3 September 1869.

41. H.S., 3 September 1869.

42. H.S., 13 August 1858, 23 August 1858, 15 October 1858, 5 November 1858.

43. H.S., 3 May 1861.

44. H.S., 26 September 1859.

45. J. St. Thomas Clarke, Report to the Urban Sanitary Authority of the Borough of Leicester, 27 August 1872, p. 6.

46. H.S., 7 November 1873.
47. *Ibid.*
48. *L.C.*, 14 December 1872; 13 November 1869.
49. *L.C.*, 9 July 1870; 13 August 1870.
50. *L.C.*, 30 December 1881.
51. *L.J.*, 9 February 1872.
52. *L.C.*, 20 January 1872.
53. Storey, *op. cit.*, p. 16.
54. *Ibid.*, p. 17.
55. *Ibid. loc. cit.*
56. *Ibid. loc. cit.*
57. *Ibid.*, p. 19.
58. J. Gordon, 'Report to the Highways and Sewerage Committee on various schemes for a Further Purification of the Sewage of Leicester'. November 1844 in the pamphlet collection of Leicester City library.
59. Storey, *op. cit.*, p. 21.
60. *L.C.*, 25 March 1899 and 20 May 1899.
61. *L.C.*, 4 April 1885 and 16 November 1889.
62. Council Minutes, 26 October 1971 and 25 January 1972.

Chapter Four

1. H.S., 14 June 1867, 8 November 1867, 20 March 1868.
2. Moore also received £5 a year as Workhouse Medical Officer, Report to Guardians, 19 March 1858, in Pamphlet, Vol. 43, in Bishop Street library.
3. H.S., 13 August 1849, and H.B., 2 May 1850.
4. Dare Report for 1849, p. 6.
5. H.B., 24 February 1847.
6. H.S., 27 July 1853.
7. *Ibid.*,
8. H.B., 29 November 1848.
9. M.O. Report, handwritten, for 5 October 1855 in L.R.O.
10. H.S., 27 February 1857.
11. H.S., 13 March 1857.
12. H.B., 20 December 1849.
13. Dr. John Snow to Parliamentary Committee on Nuisance Removal, 1855, in Irish University Press reprints of P.P.: Health General 5, paragraph 120.
14. M.O. Report, 1861, pp. 7–14.
15. *Ibid.*
16. H.S., 25 April 1862.
17. H.S., 9 May 1862.
18. H.S., 17 April 1857.
19. H.S., 15 October 1858.

20. H.S., 12 November 1858.

21. S. D. Chapman, 'The Evangelical Revival and Education in Nottingham', *Transactions of the Thoroton Society*, LXVI (1962), p. 35.

22. H.S., 8 June 1860.

23. H.S., 13 June 1860.

24. H.S., 13 July 1860.

25. H.B., 1 February 1843.

26. H.B., 20 June 1849.

27. H.S., 18 July 1856, and 1 August 1856.

28. *L.C.*, 12 November 1859.

29. *Ibid.*

30. M. Elliott, M.Phil. Thesis for University of Nottingham, 1971, on *The Leicester Board of Health 1849 to 1872*, p. 57.

31. H.S., 29 January 1858.

32. *L.J.*, 9 March 1849.

33. H.S:, 10 December 1869.

34. H.S., 3 June 1870.

35. *L.C.*, 26 August 1876; 6 January 1877; 4 November 1876; 1 July 1876; *L.J.*, 25 August 1876.

36. *L.C.*, 5 January 1878; 12 July 1879; and 19 July 1879.

37. Dare Report for 1857, p. 8.

38. H.S., 3 December 1869.

39. H.S., 12 February 1869.

40. Janet Spavold, *The Establishment and Early Years of the Leicester Police Force, 1836-46*, M.A. Dissertation for the Victorian Studies Centre Leicester University, 1970, p. 36, and *L.J.*, 11 March 1842.

41. H.S., 14 September 1860.

42. *Ibid.*

43. H.S., 15 September 1871.

44. Brian D. White, *A History of the Corporation of Liverpool 1835-1914* (1951), p. 66.

45. *Clay's Public Health Inspectors' Handbook*, 13th edition, 1972, pp. 24-5. Courses of lectures and examinations were arranged by the Royal Sanitary Institute as far back as 1877.

Chapter Five

1. M.O. Centenary Report, 1948, p. 66.

2. G. Newman, *Infant Mortality, A Social Problem* (1906), p. 42.

3. *Ibid.*, p. 47.

4. *Ibid.*, p. 48.

5. M.O., 1873, p. 8.

6. *Ibid.*

7. *L.C.*, 13 January 1872.

8. *L.C.*, 30 September 1871.

9. Dare, 1874, p. 12.

10. W. E. Buck and G. C. Franklin, *Report on the Epidemic Diarrhoea of 1875*, presented to the Sanitary Committee of the Borough of Leicester, p. 9.

11. *Ibid.*, p. 11.

12. *Ibid.*, p. 30.

13. *Ibid.*, p. 43.

14. *Ibid.*, p. 39.

15. *Ibid.*, p. 47.

16. Dr. Ballard's report quoted in M.O., 1905, p. 29.

17. Buck and Franklin, *op. cit.*, pp. 13–14.

18. Buck told the Eighth Annual congress of the Sanitary Institute in 1885 that bottle feeding was not relevant to the issue. Other speakers differed, e.g., Dr. Sweet from Liverpool thought bottle-fed babies much more vulnerable to the malady (*L.C.*, 8 January 1876).

19. G. Newman, *op. cit.*, p. 167. William Johnston was appointed Assistant M.O. in 1877 at £50 p.a. In 1879 his salary was raised to £150 p.a. By this time it was evident that Dr. Crane left most of his work to Johnston. According to one councillor: 'It had been painfully apparent for some time that Dr. Crane's advancing years unfitted him to retain the position he now held' (*L.C.*, 2 August 1879), and there was some talk of reducing his salary. In 1880 Johnston took over as M.O. at a salary of £250 p.a. The Sanitary Committee felt it better that he should retain his private practice as this added to his knowledge of various parts of the town. However, the demands of his practice grew too heavy, and he resigned in 1885. His successor, Dr. Tomkins, became the first full-time M.O.H. in Leicester at a salary of £500, for which he discharged the duties of Public Analyst, Police Surgeon and Medical Superintendent to the Fever Hospital. Professor Simmons's statement that Crane was a full-time M.O. from 1873 appears to be incorrect. (Simmons, *op. cit.*, p. 11.)

20. Newman, *op. cit.*, p. 167.

21. G. F. McCleary, *Infantile Mortality and Infants Milk Depots* (1905), p. 49.

22. M.O., 1906, p. 83.

23. M.O., 1905, p. 25.

24. Lambert, 'A Victorian National Health Service: State Vaccination, 1855–1871', *The Historical Journal*, Vol. V, No. 1, 1962.

25. Gardiner, *op. cit.*, Vol. III, p. 10.

26. *L.C.*, 22 July 1871.

27. *L.C.*, 14 February 1872.

28. *L.C.*, 23 March 1872.

29. Lambert, *op. cit.*, p. 5.

30. *L.C.*, 16 March 1872.

31. H. Hutchinson, *Jonathan Hutchinson, Life and Letters* (1946), p. 89.

32. M.O., 1866, p. 11.
33. H.S., 24 May 1872.
34. H.S., 31 May 1872.
35. *L.C.*, 5 July 1871; 16 November 1899; and Storey, *op. cit.*, p. 60.
36. M.O., 1934, p. 11.
37. *L.C.*, 5 April 1873.
38. J. T. Biggs, *Sanitation Versus Vaccination* (1912), p. 79. John Thomas Biggs was not related to the family of John and William Biggs.
39. Biggs, *op. cit.*, p. 83.
40. *Ibid. loc. cit.*
41. For Taylor, *see L.C.*, 26 June 1869, 11 December 1869, 12 March 1881, 17 September 1881, and 30 September 1881.
42. Biggs, *op. cit.*, p. 79.
43. Biggs, *op. cit.*, p. 464.
44. N. J. Frangopulo, *Rich Inheritance* (1964), p. 60.
45. M.O., 1897, p. 24.
46. *L.C.*, 13 January 1881; 2 November 1889; 6 May 1899; 18 November 1899; 16 September 1899; 16 December 1899; 6 January 1900; 10 March 1900; 16 June 1900; and I. C. Ellis, *op. cit.*, p. 57.
47. *L.C.*, 6 January 1900.
48. *The Guardian*, 29 July 1971.
49. M.O., 1934, p. 12.

Chapter Six

1. Census Report, 1871, Vol. I, p. vii.
2. E. R. Dewsnup, *The Housing Problem in England* (1907), p. 66.
3. J. Ranald Martin, *Report on the State of Nottingham and other Large Towns*: Health of Towns Commission, 1845, p. 35.
4. William Ranger, *op. cit.*, p. 10.
5. Simmons, *op. cit.*, Vol. 2, p. 10.
6. Dare Report for 1864, p. 14.
7. *Ibid.* for 1866, p. 14.
8. *Ibid. loc. cit.*
9. H.B., 24 May 1859.
10. S. D. Chapman, 'Working-Class Housing in Nottingham during the Industrial Revolution', *Transactions of the Thoroton Society*, LXVII (1963), p. 67.
11. S. D. Chapman, *The History of Working-Class Housing, A Symposium* (1971), article by J. H. Treble on 'Liverpool Working-Class Housing, 1801–61', p. 199.
12. *Ibid.*, article by M. W. Beresford on 'The Back-to-Back House in Leeds, 1787–1937', p. 102.
13. Elliott, *op. cit.*, p. 92.
14. *L.J.*, 7 September 1849.
15. *Ibid.*

16. H.S., 22 June 1853.
17. *Ibid.*
18. *Ibid.*
19. *Ibid.*
20. H.S. 31 August 1853.
21. P.R.O. MH5/8, 2 September 1853.
22. H.S., 17 March 1852. Apart from the original plan for Bland's houses in Curzon Street, this is the only instance recorded in extant building plans where the Local Board gave its consent to the erection of houses without rear entry.
23. P.R.O. MH5, correspondence of General Board of Health: letter from Samuel Stone, 6 January 1853.
24. *Ibid.*, 1 September 1853.
25. H.S., 7 September 1853.
26. H.S., 18 January 1854.
27. H.S., 15 February 1861.
28. H.S., 25 July 1862, 22 August 1862.
29. H.B., 18 December 1856.
30. *L.C.*, 15 November 1862.
31. H.S., 18 March 1864.
32. J. Barclay lecture to Leicester Literary and Philosophical Society, 1864, quoted in Colin Ellis, *op. cit.*, p. 122.
33. Dare Report for 1872, pp. 11-12.
34. Prospectus of the Leicester Freehold Land Society for 1881 in L.R.O.
35. *L.C.*, 10 October 1863.
36. Margaret Ellis, *Letters and Memorials of Eliza Ellis.*
37. *Nottingham Journal,* 1 September 1848.
38. Dare Report for 1855, p. 10.
39. Ranald Martin, *op. cit.*, p. 35.
40. T. Barclay, *Memoirs and Medleys: The Autobiography of a Bottle Washer,* p. 3.
41. *Ibid.*, p. 5.
42. *Ibid.*, p. 7.
43. *Ibid.*, pp. 9-10.
44. *The Wyvern,* 5 July 1895.
45. *L.C.*, 3 March 1888.
46. *Ibid.*
47. *L.C.*, 22 May 1897.
48. *L.C.*, 4 February 1899.
49. *L.C.*, 22 September 1900.

Chapter Seven

1. Simmons, *Leicester Past and Present,* Vol. 2, p. 12.
2. Water Company Minutes, December 1864.

3. *Ibid.*, 6 September 1865.
4. *Ibid.*, 24 October 1865.
5. Storey, *op. cit.*, p. 105.
6. Storey, *op. cit.*, p. 106.
7. H.S., 14 November 1873.
8. Mary Kirby, *Leaflets from my Life* (1887), p. 230.
9. *L.C.*, 11 November 1876; *see also* obituary, 10 December 1892.
10. *L.C.*, 28 November 1874.
11. *L.C.*, 3 April 1875; Water Company Minutes, 13 April 1870.
12. Water Company Minutes, 26 May 1854; M.O., 1856, p. 8; and 1866, p. 12.
13. *L.J.*, 9 April 1875.
14. *L.C.*, 10 April 1875.
15. *L.J.*, 16 October 1846.
16. *Ibid.*
17. *L.C.*, 4 December 1875.
18. *L.C.*, 3 April 1875; 13 February 1875.
19. *L.C.*, 20 March 1875.
20. *L.C.*, 3 April 1875.
21. *Ibid.*
22. Ranger, *op. cit.*, p. 24–5.
23. *L.C.*, 3 April 1875.
24. *Ibid.*
25. *L.C.*, 1 April 1876.
26. *L.C.*, 13 November 1875.
27. *L.C.*, 25 March 1876.
28. *L.C.*, 1 April 1876.
29. *L.C.*, 7 January 1878.
30. Storey, *op. cit.*, p. 93.
31. *L.C.*13 November 1869.
32. *L.C.*, 14 April 1877.
33. Storey, *op. cit.*, p. 96.
34. Abstracts of Accounts of the Borough of Leicester in the City Reference Library.
35. *See* table of Rates. In 1836 it was stated that the Borough Rate at a shilling a year was about half as much as poor rate (*L.J.*, 22 January 1836).
36. *L.C.*, 19 March 1881.
37. *L.C.*, 22 March 1884.
38. Water Company Minutes, 21 January 1871.
39. *Ibid.*, 10 January 1885.
40. *Ibid.*, 20 April 1855, and 11 November 1885.
41. Storey, *op. cit.*, p. 114: Relief was insufficient, however, to prevent a serious threat to the town's supply by the early 1890s. This incipient water shortage led to some ill-informed and unwarranted criticism of the Corporation by some of the London papers, including *The Builder* (*see* Simmons, *op. cit.*, Vol. 2, p. 12). The imputation of negligence was amply

refuted by Alderman Edward Wood, founder of Freeman, Hardy and Willis. He showed that the existing supplies were sufficient to meet the needs of a population well in excess of the 206,480 they supplied, while the Swithland works nearing completion would provide enough water for another 100,000 people. (*The Standard*, 21 September 1894; a copy of this letter is inserted in the Minutes of the Water committee.)

42. Storey, *op. cit.*, p. 114–5.
43. *Ibid.*, p. 117.
44. *L.C.*, 30 September 1893.
45. *L.C.*, 5 August 1899.
46. H.S., 18 August 1854.
47. M.O., 1867, pp. 9–10.
48. *L.J.*, 5 February 1847.
49. M.O., 1881, p. 37.
50. *Ibid.*, H. J. Francis, *A History of Hinckley* (1930), p. 154–5.
51. *Ibid.*
52. M.O., 1883, p. 48; 1884, p. 49.
53. M.O., 1886, p. 78; Ranger, *op. cit.*, p. 20, and M.O., 1898, p. 91.

Chapter Eight

1. Storey, *op. cit.*, p. 65.
2. *L.C.*, 21 January 1871.
3. *L.C.*, 21 January 1871.
4. *L. C.*, 18 March 1871.
5. *Ibid.*
6. *L.C.*, 11 March 1871.
7. *L.C.*, 26 July 1873.
8. H.B., 30 March 1876.
9. *L.C.*, 27 September 1879.
10. *L.J.*, 17 January 1868.
11. *L.C.*, 10 June 1871.
12. *L.C.*, 8 October 1881.
13. Town Clerk's correspondence; 26 January 1836 letter from Coventry; 16 December 1837 from Leeds; 13 November 1838 from Cambridge, etc.
14. *L.C.*, 21 February 1874.
15. *L.C.*, 28 November 1874.
16. *L.C.*, 9 November 1872.
17. *L.C.*, 29 August, 1874; 22 August 1874.
18. *L.C.*, 29 August 1874.
19. *L.C.*, 3 October 1874.
20. *Ibid.*
21. *Ibid.*
22. *L.C.*, 29 May 1875.
23. *Ibid.*, and 28 November 1874.

24. *L.C.*, 1 September 1894. By 1885 Storey had qualified as a solicitor. The offices of Town Clerk and Town Solicitor were merged and he received £1,000 p.a. for the joint salary (*L.C.*, 27 June 1885).
25. *L.C.*, 27 December 1902.
26. H.B., 23 October 1844.
27. H.S., 14 September 1853.
28. H.S., 24 September 1853.
29. H.S., 4 December 1857.
30. *L.C.*, 6 January 1872.
31. *Ibid.*
32. *Ibid.*
33. *L.C.*, 1 June 1878.
34. *Ibid.*
35. H.B., 16 November 1880.
36. *L.C.*, 11 November 1876.
37. *L.C.*, 5 June 1875.
38. *L.J.*, 12 October 1867.
39. *L.C.*, 22 June 1872.
40. Storey, *op. cit.*, p. 146.
41. *L.C.*, 6 February 1886.
42. *L.J.*, 23 April 1886, and 7 October 1882.
43. *L.C.*, 24 April 1886.
44. Storey, *op. cit.*, p. 148.
45. *L.C.*, 10 April 1886.
46. Storey, *op. cit.*, p. 163.
47. *L.C.*, 2 August 1890.
48. Storey, *op. cit.*, p. 163.
49. *Ibid.*, pp. 178–9.
50. Census returns for 1891 and 1901.
51. Simmons, *Life in Victorian Leicester*, p. 64; and Borough Accounts.
52. Flinn, *Introduction to Chadwick's Report*, p. 41.
53. *L.C.*, 3 January 1863.
54. *Ibid.*
55. Simmons, Vol. 2, p. 32.
56. *L.C.*, 13 December 1890.
57. Council Minutes, 5 February 1901, and 9 November 1899.
58. *L.C.*, 25 February 1893; 28 December 1901.
59. *L.C.*, 2 June 1900.
60. *L.C.*, 2 October 1897.
61. *L.C.*, 11 December 1897.
62. *Ibid.*
63. Simmons, *op. cit.*, Vol. 2, p. 36.
64. *L.C.*, 3 April 1875; 24 October 1885.
65. N. Pevsner, *Buildings of England: Derbyshire* (1953), p. 119. This was the Arboretum.
66. *L.C.*, 4 May 1878.

67. *L.C.*, 5 June 1875.
68. *L.C.*, 19 June 1875; 16 February 1878.
69. *L.C.*, 10 June 1882.
70. *L.C.*, 21 June 1873.
71. *L.C.*, 13 June 1885; 28 August 1886.
72. *L.C.*, 15 July 1899.
73. *L.C.*, 29 May 1897.
74. *L.C.*, 20 March 1892; 4 September 1897.
75. Read, *op. cit.*, p. 24.
76. H.B., 18 December 1856.
77. *L.C.*, 30 October 1869.
78. *L.J.*, 2 April 1841.
79. *Ibid.*
80. *L.C.*, 15 November 1845.
81. *L.C.*, 31 August 1878.
82. *L.C.*, 24 October 1896.
83. *L.C.*, 20 March 1897.
84. *L.C.*, 2 February 1895. E. P. Hennock, *op. cit.*, p. 330, notes a similar obsession for economy among I.L.P. representatives at Wolverhampton, Leeds and Manchester.
85. *The Wyvern*, 11 December 1891. Other Conservatives, however, blatantly appealed to the parsimony of ratepayers. Thus William Matts was elected to the Castle ward in 1898 on the slogan 'Vote for Matts who opposes high paid officials'. His Liberal opponent countered with the cry 'Vote for Newell and Healthy dwellings'. Matts won the seat by 12 votes. *L.C.*, 5 November 1898.
86. E. P. Hennock, *Fit and Proper Persons–Ideal and Reality in Nineteenth Century Urban Government* (1973).
87. Hennock, 'Finance and Politics in Urban Local Government in England, 1835-1900'. *Historical Journal*, VI, 2 (1963), pp. 217-8.
88. R. V. Clements, *Local Notes and the City Council* (1969), p. 160, and *passim*.
89. J. S. Mill, *Representative Government* (1912 edition), pp. 369-70.
90. Daniel Merrick, elected as a working man's candidate, *L.C.*, 14 January 1871.
91. *L.C.*, 2 February 1895.
92. H. Pelling, *Social Geography of British Elections, 1885-1910* (1967), pp. 210-11.
93. *L.C.*, 20 April 1895.
94. *L.C.*, 29 October 1898.
95. *L.C.*, 18 November 1882.
96. *L.C.*, 25 November 1882.
97. *L.C.*, 12 June 1886; 26 June 1886.
98. *L.C.*, 2 November 1895; 7 October 1899.
99. *The Wyvern*, 1 January 1892; *see also* 1.
100. Council Minutes, 1900/1, letter to Town Clerk, 29 October 1900.

INDEX